LOVING

Living with Anxiety

THE

LIFE

LESS

and how Acceptance has the Power

LIVED

to Change Your Life

About the Author

Gail Marie Mitchell has tried her hand at many things over the years from studying chemistry at the University of York to teaching in the favelas of Brazil. She now works in the exciting world of accountancy, supporting small charities in the East Midlands area. She lives in a country idyll with her husband and spends her time working, writing and trying to make sense of this crazy, confused and broken world we live in. She has lived for much of her life with anxiety and depression, conditions she has slowly learnt to accept and celebrate and which have led her to write *Loving the Life Less Lived.*

GAIL MARIE MITCHELL

LOVING

Living with Anxiety

THE

LIFE

LESS

and how Acceptance has the Power

LIVED

to Change Your Life

RedDoor

Published by RedDoor
www.reddoorpublishing.com

© 2017 Gail Marie Mitchell

The right of Gail Marie Mitchell to be identified as author of this
Work has been asserted by her in accordance with sections 77 and 78
of the Copyright, Designs and Patents Act 1988

ISBN 978-1-910453-26-1

A CIP catalogue record for this book is available
from the British Library

Cover design: Liron Gilenberg www.ironicitalics.com

Typesetting: Tutis Innovative E-Solutions Pte. Ltd

Printed and bound in Great Britain by Clays Ltd, St Ives plc.

Song lyrics on pages 60, 199 and 200 by Martyn Joseph,
all reproduced with kind permission

All statistics and information taken from the
Mental Health Foundation is reproduced with kind permission
www.mentalhealth.org.uk

Any use of the information
in this book is at the reader's discretion. It is not intended to
replace medical or psychiatric treatment or
specialist teaching methods

Dedicated to Angela Leaney
who unwittingly inspired this book – from 3500 miles away

Contents

About the Author   ii

Prologue: We're all Flashing   viii
    Tips from my Toolbox: Introducing the Toolbox   vx
    Over to You: Introducing the Toolbox   xix

1. You've Got to Have a Dream   1
    Tips from my Toolbox: Small Steps to Success   14

2. When you are Going Through Hell   23
    Tips from my Toolbox: GPs, Professional Help
    and Medication   32

3. One Woman in a Thousand   46
    Tips from my Toolbox: Let them people go   52
    Tips from my Toolbox: Music   60

4. Look Ma, No Hands   66
    Tips from my Toolbox: Eat, Move, Sleep   71

5. Count Your Blessings   90
    Tips from my Toolbox: My Positive Book   98

Contents

6. The Long Road to Healing Is Worth a
   Thousand Miracle Cures   104
      Tips from my Toolbox: Self-Help Books
      (or just books!)   111

7. Accept Who you Are but Believe Who you
   One Day Might Be   121
      Tips from my Toolbox: Acceptance   127
      Tips from my Toolbox: Cognitive Behavioural
      Therapy (CBT)   137

8. Still Crazy After All These Years   148
      Tips from my Toolbox: Coping with Panic Attacks 153
      Tips from my Toolbox: Guide for friends, family
      and colleagues   163

9. People Who Inspire: You never know how far your
   influence will reach   171
      Tips from my Toolbox: Hobbies and creativity   179

10. The Tiny Mustard Seed of Faith   188
      Tips from my Toolbox: Mindfulness   190

11. What If? And Why Not?   203
      Tips from my Toolbox: Hypnotherapy   207

12. Who Will Write the Next Chapter?   218
      Tips from my Toolbox: Build your own box of tools 222

Further Reading   235

Prologue: We're all Flashing

The day I decided to write this book I had a panic attack. There's nothing remarkable in that – in my forty-something years I have had hundreds of them, too many to mention, more than enough for it to be my 'norm'. That day was different. As usual, 'panic' took its punch, a roundhouse to my delicate self-esteem, whispering its loathsome, piteous half-truths that were guaranteed to seep through my withered defences; it went for the knock-out.

'Here we go again,' I thought, waiting for the referee's inevitable ten-second count to my defeat. 'I panic. I cry. I run away. I never go back. It has always been that way, always will be. Why would today be any different?'

It had been a strange old day, wet and wild, made for snuggling by a fire, not battling around a supermarket. Come to think of it, no Saturday was ever made for battling around a supermarket, certainly not for anyone who is followed by the Poison Panic and shadowed by the Fearful Phobia. And at that time I was strange, too. I was changing my medication and as well as the expected tearfulness, shakes and churning stomach that accompanied my every waking moment, there was a weird hypersensitivity hanging around me like an aura. I felt dizzy but at the same time hyper-alert; everything was loud but strangely distant, the lights had a migraine-inducing brightness, but it seemed like

I was somewhere else. It was a day when I should have known better than to venture out alone.

Unusually I was on my own and in a supermarket with which I was unfamiliar. I won't say its name, but it was not the orange, blue or green one – it was the yellow one. I picked up the minimal groceries I needed by deeply breathing my way around the aisles and mentally reassuring myself it would soon be over. I then headed to the checkouts. Self-checkout seemed the best option. I only had a few items and the queues at the manned tills were gridlocked. I got to a till pretty easily. I was on the home straight.

Progress is a wonderful thing, as are computers. I even celebrate self-checkouts… when they are working. That Saturday, they were most certainly not working. The first item I scanned triggered the red flashing light above the till and told me to 'please wait for assistance'. OK. No problem. I mentally comforted myself using all the therapeutic techniques I have learned over the years. There was one attendant on duty and he was very busy, but he came eventually, swiped whatever it is that they swipe and I was good to go. The second item I scanned produced more red flashing lights, more waiting for assistance. I started to breathe more deeply, trying to calm my body and mind, but my mental reassurances were becoming verbal. 'Don't panic, we're nearly there, it'll soon be over,' I found myself repeating out loud as tears streamed down my cheeks. Once more the assistant did his best to get me scanning again, but come the third item the red flashing lights started again, same for the fourth, same for the fifth. There was more waiting, with each time taking longer than the last. Each time my adrenalin rose, the world become more surreal. It was time to sob hysterically; time to run away; time to never go back. Panic had entered the ring – the undefeated heavyweight world champion. Panic would win. Panic always won.

But something was different this time. I looked at the groceries we needed for the weekend. I thought of the emotional energy I'd put in getting them from the aisles. I didn't want to go through all that again. I didn't want to have to phone my husband (who was at an important meeting or would have been with me and supporting me) and tell him there was no lunch. I didn't want to tell him that, when he'd finished his meeting, he'd have to go and get the food shopping himself while I waited in the car, unable to cope with even this simple task.

No! For the first time ever I decided that I wasn't going to roll over while Panic lifted its arms in the air and claimed another victory.

There are angels all around us. They are there when we least expect or believe in them and they come and go unaware of the profound consequences they have on people's lives. Well, maybe they're not angels, rather Good Samaritans, but in the midst of despair they feel like they are heaven sent. Today the angels were dressed as middle-aged men: one in a trench coat and panama hat, the other in a rather ordinary blue anorak. They were waiting at other malfunctioning self-checkout tills. They couldn't help but notice the tearful woman at the nearby till muttering to herself and looking as though she was about to implode. The milk of human kindness encouraged them to ask me if I was OK and if there was anything they could do to help.

'Not unless you know how to mend these machines,' I said pathetically. 'I'm having a panic attack but I'm not going to let it beat me. I'm not going to run away.' (This in itself was progress – usually by this stage my ability to speak escapes me and I'm left uttering random words like 'help' or 'want to go home'.)

The men smiled at me, not in the 'crazy-woman-let's-give-her-a-wide-berth' way I had become accustomed to over the years, but in an encouraging, almost paternal way. Somewhere in my sub conscious I felt Panic take a stumble. This was a surprise move it wasn't expecting. I wasn't expecting it either. The mouse never fights back.

'We all feel like that inside,' said the panama-hatted man.

'Yes, look, we're all flashing,' said the anoraked angel.

Panic fell back, not floored completely but definitely fazed by the newcomers who had entered the ring.

I looked around and they were right. We were all flashing. Every single self-checkout till was lit up by a red flashing bulb. If anyone should have been panicking it was the poor shop assistant who was running between us like a wasp at a barbeque trying to get the tills to cooperate.

I smiled. I think I might even have chuckled. The two men distracted me and Panic just hovered around completely uncertain of its next move.

It took an age. I still felt panicky and frightened, and frightfully embarrassed, but the kindness of strangers held my sanity together long enough to finish the shopping and pay for my goods.

Finally, an eternity later, I got back to the car carrying my groceries as though they were the spoils of war. I had achieved something! No big deal to purchase a bag of groceries. Huge deal to stick two fingers up to Panic, who had scuttled off with its tail between its legs.

I didn't know when it would be back. I never know when it is around the corner or when it will throw the next punch, but that day I learned two invaluable truths, truths which Panic and its brothers Fear and Anxiety never wanted me to hear.

First, we are all flashing. We think we are the only ones. Panic, Fear and Anxiety blinker us, lie to us and hide us from the truth. Divided we fall. But we are all flashing. We are all calling out for help (except possibly those who went to the express aisle – some people inevitably do have it easy), but there are enough of us flashing to know we are not alone. Sit on a bus, stand at a checkout, walk through a park, and at least fifty per cent of the people you see will be reaching out for something. We are not alone! You are not alone. Their demons might be drink, or pain, or grief or loneliness or depression but, if our need for help could be expressed as easily as a red light above a till, then, believe me, we'd all be flashing.

Second, I realised that day that, while my old nemesis Panic might be lurking around every corner waiting to pounce, there is also good in every situation, and sometimes a very ordinary stranger or two are right where you need them, ready to do just enough to get you through the day. So maybe they're not really angels, maybe they haven't travelled your road, they may not know your particular demons, but they are the sorts of people who have lived long enough and deeply enough to know when someone is flashing and in need of an ally.

If you are flashing and the shop assistant and the nearest friendly face seem far away – great! Be thankful you aren't on the express checkout, where it's admittedly easy but extremely boring and, believe me, nothing worthwhile, or good or soul-affirming ever happened on the expressway.

I am a failure! I had every good start in life: a good education, was comfortably well off, a high IQ. I was destined for greatness. Yet, as you will see, my story starts with me surviving on benefits on a sink estate in south Bristol, suicidal and afraid to leave the house alone. How I got there is, in some ways, irrelevant. You will have had your own 'dark days' and you will have come out the other side (or you will do – I promise), but over a period of twenty years I have learned (slowly) to be glad for the Life Less Lived. For what it has taught me, for who it has made me and for the people it has brought into my life.

'I am thankful for my struggle because without it, I wouldn't have stumbled across my strength.'

Alex Elle

A few days prior to the checkout incident an old school friend who I hadn't seen for twenty-five years tweeted a video of herself giving a talk at the Global Summit of Womensphere. Angela is now a marketing executive, she lives in the USA, flies around the world and gives talks at global summits. At school she wasn't the cleverest, prettiest or funniest person in the class. OK, she may have been up there with the leaders and high achievers, but she had no better start in life than I did. A huge voice inside my head told me not to look at this video. Not to rub salt into the wound of feeling a failure at how successful and fulfilled my classmates were compared to me. At the age of forty-five I had just left yet another job because of my anxiety issues. Did I really want to come face-to-face with how my life could have turned out if things had been a bit different?

Well of course I did. If there is a scab there, it is human nature to pick at it. I was lying in bed at the time, feeling very sorry for myself as I watched Angela's clip. She hadn't changed at all, hadn't even developed an annoying American accent (at least I could have hated her for that!). Her six-minute video talked about creating your own unique personal brand. Angela explained that we each have a unique and powerful set of skills and experiences that we can use to extend our influence and help others. She urged the women in the room to be their authentic selves and walk their own path. She said it's the things that are different about you, rather than the similarities with others, that make you memorable.

I turned the video off feeling utterly depressed and cried into my pillow. Not only was I a worthless nobody compared to my classmates (Angela had by now personified every other person I was at school with – they were all successful business women in my mind) but she was wrong! Maybe the people sitting in a conference room had a 'unique and powerful skill set,' but I didn't. All I'm good at, I thought to myself bleakly, is being anxious, worrying and messing up my life.

I thought about it a bit longer. Yep, that's definitely all I'm good at, my sorry-for-myself head told me. 'And writing,' a slightly positive voice chipped in. Feeling anxious... and writing? Yes, I have over forty years' personal experience of anxiety and mental health issues – and I quite like to write. Was it possible that this was my unique personal brand?

No – don't be ridiculous. No one wants to hear about mental health issues. Do they? And yet, according to the Mental Health Foundation, one in four people will experience mental health problems in the course of any one year, with anxiety and depression being the most common. That means that in a room of twenty people, five of them will have a mental health problem this year! Worldwide, 450 million people have a mental health problem. Views towards mental health have changed over the past twenty years but there is still a huge stigma attached to it and many people still find it embarrassing to admit to or talk about. A quick search on that large online bookstore that is so popular nowadays showed me that there are hundreds of books by so-called experts on anxiety, panic, phobias and depression, but I could count on one hand the books written by people who had actually lived through it.

One in four people will experience some kind of mental health problem in the course of a year.
Fundamental Facts About Mental Health,
Mental Health Foundation, reproduced with kind permission

So this is my story, but maybe it's your story too. If you had plans, dreams and aspirations and yet somehow illness, grief, mental ill health or just 'life' came along and robbed you of those plans, then welcome to Loving the Life Less Lived. It's time to celebrate!

It is true that, on my better days, I love my life and the new experiences my disability has brought me. I wouldn't swap places with anyone, however glamorous and exciting their life looks like from the outside. I have lived through panic attacks, suicidal periods, depression, fears, terrors and daily anxiety and I always bounce back smiling, learning and loving life more.

If you are feeling anxious, low or depressed, this book won't magically make you feel better but it will hopefully make you realise you are not alone. It might not provide any answers, although I hope you will find something useful within its pages; after all, nearly a lifetime of mental ill health has made me somewhat of an expert in the field, more than any amount of academic study could have done.

I'm not writing this book to wear my heart on my sleeve and tell you how hard done by I am. I am definitely not hard done by. Almost all of my problems have been in my head and I am sure you have experienced much worse. What I want to share with you is the lessons I have learned along the way. They won't be your lessons but I hope they will inspire you to tell your own story, to discover your own unique and authentic personality and experience, and most importantly to realise that the Life Less Lived is the best life of all.

Tips from my Toolbox: Introducing the Toolbox

I was twenty-three when I was first diagnosed with depression. At that time I knew nothing at all about mental illness and I had no tools or knowledge at all to help me deal with this. I felt the stigma radiating from me. I still remember the excruciating embarrassment of ringing my line manager and telling him I was signed off with depression; it wasn't as well publicised or widely known as it is now. I might as well have hung a bell around my neck and shouted 'unclean, unclean'.

The doctor gave me tablets and because, at that time, counselling wasn't widely available on the NHS, the number of a private therapist. These were small lifelines that gave me a little hope, but it would take many weeks of talking about my past to improve how I felt in the present. However, I didn't know what to do to get me through that day, or how to cope. I still felt empty, fearful, overwhelmed. I still wanted my life to end.

Even so, there was a determination to get better. Somewhere during this period I heard about people with chronic depression, those for who these hopeless, futile, debilitating feelings kept recurring, and I was determined to the point of obsession that that was not going to be me. I was not a weak person. I was not crazy. I was going to get better and get on with life like nothing had happened. The trouble was I had no resources – or as I now call them, tools – to prevent a relapse or to help me deal with one if it did happen again. It has taken me twenty years of self-discovery and trial and error to find out what helps and what simply makes things worse.

Everyone has 'tools' that help to get them through the day, whether we know it or not or if we call them tools. Over the years I have built up a set of useful resources that work for me. There is no one miracle cure, despite what women's magazines and TV makeover programmes would have you believe. I have found, though, that there is wisdom in most 'self-help' techniques and the trick for me has been extracting what is useful and not getting bogged down in the rest. I am not an expert in any of these fields – I have included them in each chapter only to pique your interest, in case they might work for you.

But one word of warning: A long time ago I was talking to someone who worked with drug addicts. She told me that for addicts drugs weren't the problem: they were the solution. I couldn't get my head around that. I had heard so many stories of people with 'drug problems'. What did she mean that drugs were their solution? Well I guess she meant that they started taking drugs to escape from some of the other difficulties of life, that the 'high' of taking drugs provided an escape from the situations that fate had dealt these people. The fact that drugs led them into crime, prostitution, destitution etc. was secondary to the fact that the drugs provided a release from the pain and misery they felt without them.

Illegal drugs are an extreme example of what I call 'toxic tools'. To me this is where the solution becomes as much of a problem as the original difficulty. Sometimes even more so. Alcohol is a more common example and in my teens and twenties, when I was living with mental ill health but knew very little about it and was singularly ill-equipped to deal with it, I often used excessive alcohol consumption as a tool for managing my condition. Who hasn't come home from work thinking, 'That was a stressful day – I really need a drink'? In the short term the drink has a calming effect and makes you feel good. So what if the next day you have a headache and feel groggy and a bit fed up – it was worth it. It is then easy to slip into having a few drinks three, four, five nights a week... then you don't just fancy a drink – you *need* a drink. It starts to cost more money, it becomes a dependency, more and more headaches, weight gain, a growing sense of self-loathing. Yes, I've been there! Before and after the time of my first diagnosis I regularly drank to oblivion to hide from the black hole of despondency inside me. I'm not saying everyone who drinks most days is an alcoholic, or even that they should stop. Everyone is responsible for their own actions. However, it is worth considering the question: 'Is this helping or is it adding to the problem?'

Even seemingly innocuous 'solutions' can become problems if taken to an extreme. I've used retail therapy to give myself a mental boost. That may be OK if you can afford it, but my credit card balance just grew and grew and the 'things' I purchased never did anything to block the blackness I was feeling inside. I ate (still eat) when I was angry, when sad, when worried, when depressed. I 'treated' myself with donuts and chips and yet I knew I was (and still am) morbidly obese and that sugars and fats did not nourish my body and certainly didn't help my mental state.

These are just a couple of my own toxic tools, but there are many more. Maybe drugs and self-harm are extreme examples, but even seemingly healthy solutions can become toxic. Take my unusual personal solution of cleaning the house. This could easily become an obsession with germs, and take over the ability to relax; exercise can become an 'addiction', pushing the body to the limits; friendships that were once nourishing can become parasitic. I believe it is important to periodically review your toolbox and ask: 'Is this helping or is it adding to the problem?'

Throughout this book I will give an insight into my toolbox and show what has worked for me. My tools will change, as I find new ways of dealing with anxiety or outgrow some of the old methods. When I was twenty-three there was no internet, few books about mental health problems and little publicity. I felt like a pariah groping about in the dark. If some of my tools and experiences can shed a little light for someone else sitting in a cold office ringing the Samaritans in an attempt to save themselves from their own inner terrors, it will have been worth the journey.

Important warning: These tools have all worked for me over a long period of time. They are not quick-fix solutions and are no substitute for professional intervention. If you are in crisis and feel you can't go on, ring a doctor and get an emergency appointment. Then ring the Samaritans and/or a trusted and supportive friend. I believe the ideas in this book can and will help you over time, but they are not intended as a crisis-management tool.

- If you are in crisis at this moment, call for help! Ring your GP, the NHS, a helpline like the Samaritans or a trusted friend.

Phone numbers in the UK
- NHS   111
- Samaritans   116 123

Over to You: Introducing the Toolbox

This section is all about you! Throughout this book I will share the tools I have found to be most effective for me, but at the end of each toolbox session I will include some pointers as to how you can get these tools to work for you and where you can go to find more detailed information. This first 'over to you' section gives you a chance to think about which tools you already use and how helpful those tools are in the long term.

- Think about all the tools you use to cope with your anxiety, depression, pain or low mood. It might help to write them down.
- Next to each item on the list write down whether each tool is helping the situation or adding to the problem.
- Some tools might be both useful and harmful either because of the degree to which you use them (e.g. one chocolate bar might give you the lift you need, eating lots of chocolate on a regular basis can cause weight gain, blood sugar imbalances, guilt and so on) or because of the nature of the particular tool (e.g. spending time with some people can really boost your mood while other friends can drag you down to the brink of despair).
- For now it is enough of a step to become aware of the tools you reach for and to take time to consider their usefulness or otherwise. **Remember to ask: Is this helping or adding to the problem?**
- Gradually focus your efforts on the tools that are helping in both the short and long term. As you read this book you

will learn about the tools that have worked for me; they may not work for you but I hope they will give you food for thought. It is not an exhaustive list, just what I have found on my journey so far.

- If you identify tools that are causing a problem, stop using them. Easier said than done I know, and if they are not easy to give up that could be a clue to the fact that they are harmful or addictive. If you can't do it yourself get help, either by asking your GP or finding a support group. I just googled 'Anonymous UK' and it came up with a host of organisations from Cocaine Anonymous UK (www.cauk. org.uk) to Overeaters Anonymous UK (www.oagb.org. uk) and many things in between. Whatever your particular toxic tool you can guarantee that someone has been there before… and found a way to overcome it.

- **Knowing you need help and asking for it is a strength, not a weakness.**

CHAPTER ONE

You've Got to Have a Dream

In September 2001, at exactly the same time that the world was being shocked by events in New York, my mum was on holiday in San Francisco. From that holiday she brought home possibly the best present she has ever given me, although at the time I, rather ungratefully, thought it was cheap tat. It was a laminated photo of the Golden Gate Bridge which probably only cost a couple of dollars, and there were a million and one other things I needed at that point. Yet I still have that picture on my kitchen wall to this day. It's not pretty or tasteful and it doesn't fit with my colour scheme but it means the world to me.

Five years before that day, I had been a chartered accountant, fully qualified, working at the head office of a multinational company, with a brilliant and successful career assured. Admittedly I'd had a bout of depression in my early twenties, but I was sure I was cured of all that. I lived in the most beautiful Georgian house in a trendy part of Bristol. I was approaching my thirties and it seemed like the world was my oyster. Everything was going to plan.

By the time my mum gave me this magical present, my meteoric fall to earth, which had taken only a few years, was well established and seemingly irreversible. I had had to sell my beautiful home and move to a dilapidated semi in Knowle West, a notorious council estate in the south of the city. The first time I'd ever heard of Knowle West I was new to Bristol and with some friends on a summer evening when we saw a fire on a hill in a different part of the city. It turns out it was the school at Knowle West which had succumbed to an arson attack. None of the Bristolians were surprised by this; it seemed to them a perfectly normal occurrence for that part of the city, which was known for its riots, high unemployment and criminal activity. When I moved there it had improved even though the local shop still hid all its wares behind bullet-proof Perspex and graffiti brightened up every spare space of grey concrete.

Although I had done my best to do the house up, funds were low and my only income was incapacity benefit. That might not have been so bad; I did have a roof over my head and I met some wonderful people during my time in Knowle West. The real problem was the state of my mind. I was petrified of pretty much everyone and everything. I hated leaving the house alone, I believed my life was over, and there was a stream of locations I would never (and still have never wanted to) return to because they were the sites of some of my frequent, debilitating and very embarrassing panic attacks.

Mum handed me the unimpressive gift and I tried to look appreciative. She always put a lot of thought into buying gifts and this one was no exception. In fact it is the meaning she attached to this memento, and the thought of her lovingly packing it into her suitcase and bringing it to me knowing I was prone to turning my nose up at her crazy schemes and ideas that makes it so precious to me now. 'This is your challenge,' Mum said. I was sceptical about what was coming next, a challenge was the last thing I needed. 'One day you will visit the Golden Gate Bridge,' she beamed at me as though she had prescribed the answer to all my problems.

I looked at her as if she was crazy! 'But Mum,' I said, 'I can't even go to Tesco on my own. How can I ever get to the Golden Gate Bridge?'

'You will,' she said. 'I believe in you.'

I believed she was bonkers! But I still stuck the picture up in my kitchen, probably only so as not to offend her, but something about that challenge kept niggling away at the back of my mind.

After my mum's visit I lay in bed feeling very sorry for myself (a frequent theme throughout my life), wondering how things had come to this. I sobbed pitifully and scolded myself for letting my life spiral so far out of control. How had it happened?

* * *

I had had a fortunate middle-class upbringing. My home life hadn't been perfect, but then again, whose is? I was an awkward and shy child, afraid of grown-ups and preferring my own company, but it was nothing that would strike you as odd. Shortly after I had started school at five years old, my mum walked past the playground at lunchtime to check I was OK. I didn't see her but, many times over the next few years, she would tell the story of how I was sitting alone playing by myself while all the other children were enjoying each other's company.

This really upset my mum and at the age of five I could never understand why. I was happy playing on my own, I didn't feel rejected by the other children – in fact I can't even remember the incident – but in my mum's eyes being popular and having lots of friends were marks of 'normality'. I think she probably guessed then and there that I wasn't ever going to turn out 'normal'.

Despite that one incident I had many friends growing up and I was fortunate to go to a good grammar school. It was not the best school in the country, but for a non-fee paying school it had excellent results and I thrived there. To attend, you had to pass the eleven-plus and my primary school teacher had advised my parents not to put me in for it, saying I didn't stand a chance. Luckily they didn't listen, and probably the reason I didn't show my full potential at primary school was that I was afraid of my teacher! I felt so proud when the letter came to say I had been accepted at Chelmsford County High School for Girls. I had succeeded at something. My parents were proud of me! I remember them buying me a royal blue tracksuit and a fountain-pen set for my achievements. This was a hugely pivotal moment in my life. A chance to 'make something of myself.'

I loved that school from the second I arrived to the day I left seven years later. I felt like I was at Enid Blyton's Malory Towers and I did well, getting good exam results, not the best – a couple of Bs in with all the As – but enough to get into a good university to study chemistry. Everything was going according to plan. Come to think of it, I'm not sure I had a plan at that point – if I did, it vaguely consisted of having a career and being a success and making my parents proud. I'm glad I didn't know then how far short of all those aims I would fall by the age of thirty.

* * *

Back in my pit of gloom a dozen years later, tears streamed down my face as I remembered the promise and potential that my early life had showed. It hurt to remember happier times but, even in my deepest despair, I think I was always preparing myself to climb back out of the mire. I just didn't know how to do it. The demons inside my head were so real, telling me I was worthless, useless, a bad person… I screamed, sobbed and tortured myself with thoughts of how and when the rot had set in.

* * *

I'd always been an anxious and quiet child. My mum said I had a miserable face and was always telling me to smile and look like I was enjoying myself. I can't remember ever *not* enjoying myself, or ever really feeling miserable as a child, but I was always nervous around grown-ups and never quite knew what to say or how to act. I suppose the difficulties began to show when I started university – now I *was* a grown-up, but inside I still felt like a kid. I found studying stressful and I guess you would've called me 'highly strung' if you'd known me at the time. But at least university was a safe environment – I started to get scared when I thought about leaving the campus and joining the outside world.

I was at a complete loss when it came to deciding on a career path. I didn't know what I wanted to do or what I'd be good at. In the end I chose chartered accountancy in the mistaken belief that I wouldn't have to deal with people. That was the sum of my whole decision-making process! Pick the job with the least contact with other people! If lighthouse keeper or hill sheep farmer had been on offer I would probably have picked them instead!

I had a beautiful suit for my interviews, a tailored jacket and a wrap-over skirt in dark grey, matched with a cream silk blouse. I must have felt confident and come across that way as I was offered six jobs. Six jobs as a trainee chartered accountant! If that didn't boost my confidence nothing would.

I took a job in Nottingham with one of the biggest accountancy firms in the world, and I managed for several years, passing all my exams and qualifying quickly. I don't know how I appeared on the surface, but inside I was struggling. It didn't feel right. I didn't feel right. It was like everyone else knew what they were doing but I was just pretending. The underlying anxiety was exhausting and, looking back, something was going to give. I kept thinking somebody soon was going to notice I was faking it.

'I'm not different for the sake of being different, only for the desperate sake of being myself. I can't join your gang: you'd think I was a phony and I'd know it.'

Vivian Stanshall

The first time mental illness reared its ugly head I was twenty-three. Nothing had changed from the preceding years; it was just that the fears, feelings and experiences I had lived with in childhood were growing louder and brighter, leading to a crescendo of chaos and turmoil.

I had nothing to worry or despair about at that time in my life. I was working for an international firm of accountants, one of the best in the world. I had a degree, a relationship, friends and a reasonable income, with the promise of much higher earnings when I qualified. As far as my career was concerned the sky was the limit. I had a good social life and was just starting out on an independent, successful and exciting life.

So why did I want to kill myself?

Depression

The term 'depression' is used to describe a range of moods, ranging from low spirits to more severe mood problems that interfere with everyday life. Symptoms may include a loss of interest and pleasure, excessive feelings of worthlessness and guilt, hopelessness, morbid and suicidal thoughts, and weight loss or weight gain. A depressive episode is diagnosed if at least two out of three core symptoms have been experienced for most of the day, nearly every day, for at least two weeks. These core symptoms are:

- Low mood
- Fatigue or lack of energy
- Lack of interest or enjoyment in life

A depressive episode may be classed as mild, moderate or severe, depending on the number and intensity of associated symptoms, such as sleep disturbance, appetite and weight change, anxiety, poor concentration, irritability and suicidal thoughts.

Between 8% and 12% of the population experience depression in any year.

Fundamental Facts About Mental Health,
Mental Health Foundation, reproduced with kind permission

It's a long time ago now – there isn't much I remember about the build-up of emptiness inside me, but I clearly recall finding a quiet office at work and ringing the Samaritans in a desperate attempt to share with someone how I was feeling. An hour later I was in the GP's surgery being diagnosed with depression.

I was stunned. To me, depression meant straitjackets, padded cells and intolerable unending blackness. It was what happened to weak people, crazy people: surely if I was depressed I should be rocking and staring at walls somewhere in the depths of a grim mental hospital?

So I was diagnosed with this mystery illness, depression, which I knew nothing about. I had several months off work, took anti-depressant medication, received private counselling (there wasn't much available on the NHS back then) and hid from the world. But that brief dip didn't halt my career success. I was promoted, I got a better job, I was relocated to Bristol and everyone seemed to think I was a rising star destined for bigger and greater things. What could they see that I couldn't? Why did I feel such a phoney? What was happening on the outside of my life just didn't match the reality that existed in my head. I felt sick going to work every day and was anxious over every tax computation I calculated, every phone call I made or every business meeting I attended. I was permanently stressed out and depressed. I worried over every conversation I had, every facial expression pulled by others, exhausted by the emotional strain of not crying and screaming. At the time I didn't know it was an illness. It was just the way I was.

I could have carried on that way for years – or at least until I had a breakdown. I self-medicated with alcohol (one of my toxic tools) to give myself at least some relief from the interminable fear, dread and worry that I kept hidden from view. Maybe I thought I could keep it hidden forever, but part of me was desperately looking for an escape route. It was easy to blame work for the way I felt. It was a stressful job, with long hours and lots of responsibility. I reasoned with myself that I was perfectly ordinary; there was nothing wrong with me. It was the job that was driving me insane. It was the job, not me, that was to blame.

It was the job, not me, honest!

Eventually, at the age of twenty-eight, I made the decision to quit my job and 'take a sabbatical'. My rational mind reasoned that accountancy wasn't for me, I didn't agree with the ethics of it, I wanted to 'find myself', but the truth was I was running scared. I didn't know how long I could carry on, I felt like a fish out of water. For the first (but definitely not the last) time in my life, I ran away.

* * *

For many people low mood and anxiety go hand in hand, but I was never stuck in the inertia of depression for very long. My anxiety, self-loathing and perfectionism would always drive me to find solutions to my current predicament. Even if my 'current predicament' was rock bottom. Even if the 'solutions' included the option of suicide. Having exhausted myself with tears after mum's visit back in 2001, and haunted myself with memories of more positive times, I fell into a deep sleep and woke up several hours later in the befuddled and groggy state that comes with daytime sleeping. As I came to consciousness that familiar feeling of dread, which accompanied most of my waking hours, took hold in the pit of my stomach. I felt wretched and hated myself for ruining my life and hurting my family.

I forced myself to shower and make a strong black coffee and, as I was pouring the water into the cafetière, I caught a glimpse of the laminated picture of the Golden Gate Bridge that mum had thoughtfully brought for me and which I had reluctantly pinned to the fridge. 'San Francisco indeed!' I thought to myself. 'That's ridiculous!'

Sipping my coffee on the sofa and wondering which soaps were on that evening that might help take my mind off my self-pity, I couldn't move away from the challenge Mum had given me. Obviously it was out of my league (and price range), but did I really want this to be my reality for the rest of my life? Living on benefits, afraid of my own shadow, sick and fearful every waking moment and achieving nothing with each day that passed. Not that I hadn't grown to love my house, and even the estate it was situated on. I craved solitude at the time and I had it in abundance, so why would I pressure myself to step out of my comfortable cocoon? No, I would sit here and watch *Corrie*, and I would be fine!

Although not having any money was a pain…

No… it was too scary to contemplate any other existence. *Corrie* first and then *EastEnders*!

But just think how much I'd let my family down and how worried they were about me…

Not listening… it's my life! They don't need to worry about me – I'm safe here! OK so there are rumours that a drug dealer lives in the house opposite but they're not bothering me. I can shut the curtains, shut out the world, turn the phone off…

* * *

I remember vividly the first time I realised I had bigger mental health problems than I had ever previously imagined and that my inner demons were not going to leave me alone so easily. After leaving accountancy I had no real plan of where I was going or what I wanted to do. I wanted to find a 'direction' in life. Up until that point everything had been mapped out for me and, even though I had felt like I was going the wrong way up a dual carriageway at 100 mph, it was still a guided journey – school – uni – professional qualification – get promoted – earn lots of money… Now I was in the middle of a wilderness with no compass, and GPS hadn't even been invented yet!

I signed up for a year of theology study at Bristol Baptist College, more to find a map for my life and rest my exhausted mind than to gain any sort of ecclesiastical qualification. I didn't find any direction, not that year anyway, but I did find myself and I really didn't like what I discovered.

Bristol Baptist College at that time was in an ancient but magnificent building which could have reminded me of a smaller version of Hogwarts if any of the Harry Potter books had been published at the time. It was a safe place, full of Christian good intention, but it was also a minefield where I was out of my depth and where my faith in everything from God to my own sanity was shattered to the core. Looking back, that wasn't such a bad thing: faith without questioning isn't faith, it is just blind ignorance.

I remember spending many hours crying in that first year, which was new for me. I had reigned in my pent-up emotions for year after year, maintaining the façade of being a 'normal' person and now, in the middle of this wilderness, they spilled out in abundance. That wasn't so terrible. I did then, and still do, see crying as a therapeutic tool that is more a restorative balm than a sign of weakness.

No, the real sign that something was wrong began one mealtime. Meals were a communal affair at the college, served in the beautiful dining room at long oak tables. The college was small, probably only forty students and staff, and I valued the companionship of these mealtimes even though at heart I was a solitary figure and I found many of the theological debates that accompanied the repast upsetting and far beyond my understanding.

I have no recollection of what sparked the incident which is etched indelibly in my brain, but I know I was helping with the washing up after one meal with seven or eight others in the small kitchen. For some reason, without any discernible trigger, I started screaming, loud and long at the top of my voice. Why? I don't know. And I don't mean a small shriek or a half-hearted squeal: it was a deep, loud, gut-wrenching yell that lasted several minutes but seemed to go on for an eternity. How I stopped or got back to my room I can't remember. But in that pivotal moment of my life it felt like the hounds of hell had reached up through my soul and were torturing the very essence of my being.

I had no understanding of my emotions. They seemed to come from outside of myself and attack me. I was out of control and screaming in public! Wasn't that the sort of thing mad people did? Especially as, for the life of me, I can remember no cause for it. I was scared out of my wits. I was scared of myself. The one thing I couldn't, and still can't, run from is myself. I knew I should be locked up, certified insane, sectioned, put in a straitjacket. I felt like a crazy person. How could I ever get past this hugely alarming, not to mention embarrassing, moment?

Social phobia, a persistent fear of being seen negatively or humiliated in social or performance situations, is the third most commonly diagnosed mental disorder in adults worldwide, with a lifetime prevalence of at least 5%.

Generalised anxiety disorder (GAD) is diagnosed after a person has on most days for at least six months experienced extreme tension (increased fatigue, trembling, restlessness, muscle tension), worry, and feelings of apprehension about everyday problems. The person is anxious in most situations, and there is no particular trigger for anxiety.

Fundamental Facts About Mental Health,
Mental Health Foundation, reproduced with kind permission

I spent several weeks following that incident hiding in my room; my meals were brought to me and I would only venture to the communal bathroom if I was sure that no one was about. I was referred to a psychiatrist at the Bristol Royal Infirmary who prescribed medication, and I have taken medication every day for nearly twenty years since. He diagnosed 'social phobia'. Later I would also be diagnosed with 'generalised anxiety disorder'.

Having a name for it helped. At least the psychiatrist hadn't said I was mad! Maybe they teach them not to say that at Psychiatrists' School. He even seemed to think it was all right to let me out in public. I personally didn't feel safe out in public, so I buried myself away in one small room at college, feeling the failure and despair of my existence and afraid that those disturbing and all-consuming emotions might batter down my defences again.

* * *

The Golden Gate Bridge photo stared at me accusingly as I made my breakfast the next morning. I felt the familiar stone of dread and fear in my stomach, which was so ingrained in me that it felt like a physical part of my anatomy, a third arm: I felt something was wrong if it ever left. But I felt rested after a good night's sleep, and a coffee lifted me a little more. The photo continued to stare. I couldn't bring myself to put it in the bin. What did I have to do today? No doctor's appointments, no visits from anyone, not much on the TV. My life had condensed into getting through the next hour without a panic attack. Was this to be my existence for the next fifty years? I could do some tidying and watch some daytime TV: safe enough pursuits. I didn't have to see anyone, which was a relief. Seeing people always threatened to tip my underlying anxiety over into panic.

Did I really have any control over my condition? At that time, apart from medication, I had very few tools to help me through the day. Hiding was my biggest tool. The further I could get from people the better I felt. Running away was another of my best lines of defence. If I did venture out and get out of my depth I could run away back to the sanctuary of my little run-down semi. I knew these solutions weren't so much answers and that they actually added to my problems, but I had no idea how to change. I knew I was never going to get to San Francisco, it was a hopeless pipe dream, but something about what Mum had said made me determined (albeit in a half-hearted, slightly pathetic way) that my life could be more than this. I fetched some coloured pens and paper and began to plan. For five years my life had had no direction – now I was tentatively beginning to draw a map. It wasn't a map to California, but it was possibly going to take me a little way down the road, out of my comfort zone, and maybe towards a more socially acceptable existence.

Tips from my Toolbox: Small Steps to Success

How do you eat an elephant?
One bite at a time.

Traditional proverb

Maybe you know this feeling, but just about every single morning I wake up with the sword of Damocles hanging over my head. Fear and dread of the day ahead fill my first waking thoughts, even if the day ahead only entails pottering around the house doing things I enjoy; in fact, often my fears are worse when I am 'supposed' to be relaxing. My subconscious mind has, overnight, been reminding me of all the hidden obstacles which could appear, and I have invariably been plagued by dreams of apocalyptic scenes, death and calamity. I regularly wake up screaming (which has caused great alarm to house guests and probably the neighbours as well!). At least two mornings a week I awake with a pounding headache that encompasses my shoulders, neck and upper back, probably caused by the tense state my REM sleep has brought me to. Does any of this sound familiar to you?

These feelings hit me before any conscious thought can reach my mind and, even by the time I have reassured myself that there really is nothing to be frightened of in the day ahead, my body is on full 'fight or flight' alert – after all, something could go wrong! Who knows when Damocles' sword will fall?

In case you are wondering who on earth Damocles is and what's all this about his sword I will try and briefly paraphrase the Greek legend. Damocles was a great and powerful ruler who appeared to have all the fortune and wealth any man could want. One of his courtiers asked to swap places with Damocles so that he, the courtier, could experience that fortune and wealth first-hand. Damocles agreed, but over the head of his throne he placed a sword that was held in place by only a single horse's hair. The courtier soon begged to swap back to his original place in society, realising that with great power and fortune comes also fear and anxiety and the ever-present threat of danger.

I'm not powerful, although I am very fortunate, so am I alone in carrying around a fear that at any minute the sword could drop? Maybe. Maybe if I had real hardship and persecution to occupy my mind I wouldn't be so afraid? Who knows? I am who I am, where I am, and this is what I live with.

So how do I get up and get through the day?

Small steps!

In the hilariously funny 1991 film *What About Bob?* Richard Dreyfuss's character is a psychiatrist who has made a name for himself with his book *Baby Steps*. If you've ever seen the film you will know that he's a terrible psychiatrist, but I love his idea of baby steps. He explains: 'It means setting small, reasonable goals for yourself. One day at a time, one tiny step at a time – do-able, accomplishable goals. Baby steps. When you leave this office, don't think about everything you have to do to get out of the building, just deal with getting out of the room. When you reach the hall, just deal with the hall. And so forth. Baby steps.'

> It means setting small, reasonable goals for yourself. One day at a time, one tiny step at a time – do-able, accomplishable goals. Baby steps.
>
> *What About Bob?* 1991

Which is exactly what I try to do when the fear and anxiety threatens to overwhelm me. I don't think about everything I have to achieve that day, week, lifetime; I try not to dwell on every possible disastrous scenario that could play out during the next twenty-four hours. I just say to myself, 'OK, I'll just get up and make a coffee and see how I feel then.' Usually after a coffee I can then persuade myself to get dressed having managed to distract myself with some inane and mindless breakfast television. The caffeine has given me a quick shot in the arm and once I'm dressed I can look at what needs doing for the day. As a rule, I start by picking a small job that is easily completed and ticked off. Which again will give me another boost. By 11 a.m. I tend to be feeling more confident in my ability to cope with the world we live in and life in general.

Maybe you are familiar with baby steps, too; if not I guarantee you will find the idea useful if life (or even just the day ahead) seems overwhelming. The first time in my life I employed 'small steps' was that morning in 2001 after Mum had deposited the 'Golden Gate Bridge Challenge' on my doorstep/ fridge. I didn't know it as small steps then. I didn't realise that this was my first attempt at finding ways to get out of my angst-filled prison, but looking back this was the first effort I had ever made to consciously improve my situation and take control of my life.

I sat down at the kitchen table with a rainbow of felt-tip pens, very little hope and the picture of San Francisco bearing down on me from the fridge. I still have the list I wrote. I keep it as a memento of how far I have come, my very first Small Steps to Success Plan. Down the left-hand side I have written 'level of difficulty' and down the right there is a tick list with the heading 'achieved'. At the top of the list are easy challenges:

Small Steps to Success Plan

Difficulty	Activity	Achieved?
1.	Invite Kathryn to my house	Yes
2.	Go to the cinema with Clare	Yes
3.	Telephone Debbie	Yes
After a while the list built up to more scary propositions…		
17.	Group night out with friends	
18.	Answer the phone without looking at caller ID	
The list climaxed with horrendously scary, unthinkable tests at the bottom…		
30.	Join a new group filled with strangers	
31.	Go into a shop and complain	
32.	Face up to people I have previously run away from	

As I say, this was my first attempt at small steps. In hindsight I built up far too quickly to more frightening propositions, some of which I have still never achieved fifteen years later! The point is I had something to aim for and I achieved much more than I probably would have done if I'd sat staring at the picture on my fridge bemoaning the woes of my life.

Nowhere on my list was there any proposal to leave Bristol, or leave the country and fly to America unaccompanied, or even contemplate getting a job, but something about ticking off these small steps must have given me confidence to aim higher because within a year I had a part-time job (albeit with my own personal support worker employed to help me cope) and a little bit more hope about the future, although there was still a very long way to go.

To this day I use very similar techniques to get me through difficult days and big challenges. My range of coloured pens has increased, as has my ability to know what is a positive step and what is a leap too far. I'm a great fan of lists and, although I can sometimes become a slave to them and they can turn into a toxic tool, they are also a great way to manage my small baby steps. Lists help me see what must be done and what can be left for a day when I feel stronger. Lists reduce the fear that there is something really important I should be doing that I've forgotten about. I add feel-good nourishing activities to my list as well – which I should probably be able to do spontaneously, but it helps to see them in black and white and, if I really can't face any of my jobs, sometimes ticking off 'walk', 'shower' or 'read a novel' can be therapy enough to boost my mood.

A friend once told me that 'you can do anything for fifteen minutes.' I'm not sure that's true; I certainly couldn't jog for fifteen minutes! But the principle of breaking an unsurmountable task down into manageable chunks has certainly helped me function on many a day when I felt like hiding under the duvet crying and shivering in dread. Inevitably, once I get going, and have completed a few baby steps, I realise things aren't anywhere near as bad as I had imagined. The sword of Damocles doesn't seem so deadly, and I have a few drops more confidence to move forward and face what lies ahead.

Over to You: Your Own Small Steps to Success

- Decide what you want to achieve. It may be a short-term aim like getting out of bed and making it to lunchtime or a longer-term goal like getting back into work. Small steps to success will work equally well for any goal.

- Make a list (mental or written) of all the small steps you can take along the way.
- Focus on the first small step and get started on it. Don't worry how you will finish it, don't think about steps two to thirty. Just get started on step one.
- Do step one for fifteen minutes.
- If that's all you can cope with then that's fine; have a rest and come back to your list at a later time.
- Congratulate yourself.
- Think you can do more? Continue with step one for another fifteen minutes, then another until you can tick that off your list.
- Congratulate yourself.
- Keep going, one small step at a time.

DO NOT, I repeat, DO NOT skip over the congratulating yourself part. (I'm being bossy now and I'm not a bossy person despite what those closest to me say.) Even if the task you've just completed is something most people take for granted it doesn't mean it's easy for you. There are many people who find getting out of bed/going into a supermarket/opening an official letter a mammoth task. You are not alone; you have drawn on your reserves of courage and strength and you deserve a huge pat on the back and maybe a nice mug of tea for your efforts.

Potential Tool	Helps in the short term	Helps in the long term	Causes problems	Never tried
Avoiding people/ situations				

Potential Tool	Helps in the short term	Helps in the long term	Causes problems	Never tried
Avoiding going out				
Bingeing				
Cleaning				
Cognitive Behavioural Therapy				
Competitive sports				
Counselling				
Creative hobby				
Drinking alcohol				
Eating healthily				
Eating unhealthily				
Gardening				
Hypnotherapy				
Illegal drugs				
Keeping busy/ never relaxing				
Legal highs				

Potential Tool	Helps in the short term	Helps in the long term	Causes problems	Never tried
Listening to music				
Mindfulness				
Prayer/spiritual support				
Prescribed medication				
Reading				
Rituals				
Self-harm				
Self-help books				
Sleep				
Spending time with friend a…				
Spending time with friend b…				
Spending time with friend c…				
Support from GP				

Potential Tool	Helps in the short term	Helps in the long term	Causes problems	Never tried
Support from other professional (CPN/ therapist)				
Walking/ running				
Watching TV				
Writing				

CHAPTER TWO

When you are Going Through Hell

In 2012 there were 5,981 deaths by suicide in the UK. In 2012, 21% of contacts with Samaritans (over 600,000) involved individuals expressing suicidal feelings.

Samaritans Suicide Statistics Report 2014

I am acutely aware that many of the incidents and scenarios I describe in this book have a comical and slightly ludicrous air to them. Looking back, and for you looking on, it's easy to laugh at the absurdity of it all and to see that just a small change in thought or action could have made a huge difference in how I felt or indeed how things turned out.

How can I describe how debilitating, all-consuming and soul-destroying these fears and panics are at the time they are occurring? They are irrational but they are extremely real, and re-living them now I can still feel the physical pain and discomfort they caused me. Maybe if you've been through similar experiences you will understand. However, I know that I am speaking a foreign language when I try and explain it to many people out there.

Charlie Chaplin said that life is tragedy when seen in close-up but a comedy in long-shot. That is so true! I believe wholeheartedly that we must see the funny side – in hindsight. However, to be able to laugh and shrug things off when the wild animals of panic and anxiety are crowding in from every side, how can we do that?

'Life is a tragedy when seen in close-up, but a comedy in long-shot.'

Charlie Chaplin

And what if we are so exhausted, so worn down, so depressed by either our circumstances or our emotions that we feel there is no way out? That there is no room for laughter or looking on the bright side, or seeing that tomorrow is another day?

Anxiety has always been my 'issue' and for a long time it seemed to me that anxiety and depression were polar opposites and I couldn't understand how they could so often be diagnosed together. Now I realise that they are just different sides of the same coin. The despair and fatigue of overwhelming, never-ending anxiety can certainly be depressing. The fear of absolutely everything can often lead to the belief that life is not worth living. That it would be better to prepare an exit plan. In truth there have been many times in my life when suicide has not merely seemed like a solution but it has appeared to be the *only* solution.

Please don't get the impression that getting that picture of the Golden Gate Bridge from my mum initiated some sort of Damascus Road experience which turned my life around and everything was uphill from that moment. Far from it. I'd had many long dark tortuous and suicidal days up to that point and I was to have many more after. However, that picture gave me something to aim for even if, back then, it seemed impossible that I would one day have the courage to get on a plane and travel to a tourist destination on the other side of the world. Far beyond the Golden Gate were goals that at the time I couldn't even form into words: aims like living without the recurring sensation of wanting to end my life, ideas of maintaining a loving relationship or of working full-time in a job that I enjoyed and found worthwhile. These ambitions were as far beyond me as a journey to the centre of the sun.

I couldn't voice them, or add them to a Small Steps to Success list or even admit them to myself because I would then be faced with the truth that these things which so many take for granted belonged in a parallel universe. To admit I was aiming for San Francisco was, at the time, a ridiculous and unattainable enough dream for me.

Anxiety has been with me every day of my life. I can remember as a child worrying about many things and feeling overwhelmed by them. One school report described me as 'dour'. That was in the days before caring-sharing teachers, when dour was a criticism rather than a symptom that something was wrong. As a child of about five or six a classmate put a 'spell' on me and told me that when I was sixteen I would die. I was horrified and extremely worried. I lay awake night after night petrified that I would die young. In fact I continued to panic about that, off and on, until my seventeenth birthday! It never occurred to me to discuss the rationality of it with a teacher or a parent!

Even now when I'm at my best, when I'm coping well, I maybe worry about fifty things a day, although often the worries fly through my brain faster than I can process them. I am simply left with the feeling of sickness in my stomach, tension in my chest and tears in my eyes, never quite remembering what thought or incident brought me to that state. That's a good day, a day when, if you met me, you wouldn't know there was anything wrong. Sitting here I cannot remember a time when I have been completely calm and without worry, although I know there have been a few, maybe on ordinary days when I wasn't trying to be happy and peace took me unawares. If I could remember them there wouldn't be enough to count on the fingers of one hand.

I don't even get relief when I am asleep. Even at the best of times I dream constantly and vividly, waking up with my mind racing. Whether well or ill I probably wake up screaming from a nightmare at least twice a week, sometimes as often as twice a night. I frequently dream of being chased by Nazis, aliens or monsters. I dream of nuclear wars or other apocalyptical events. Worse by far are the dreams set in everyday situations where everyone – my colleagues, family, friends – is shouting at and criticising me. I wake up exhausted and emotionally drained several times a week, with a splitting headache and tension down my back and neck. One plus point is that I am quite often very glad to have woken up as then 'real' life doesn't seem so bad at all.

Nowadays I have tools and techniques to deal with most of these symptoms. In my twenties and early thirties, I had some medication from a GP and a pathetic-looking little list written in coloured felt-tip pen. No job, no money, no prospects and worst of all, no hope.

Imagine (although I'm sure many of you don't need to imagine – I am definitely not alone in this) being followed around by someone who constantly calls you stupid, or a failure. Who tells you that you are hateful, unlovable, disgusting. For many years I spoke to myself in a way I would never speak to another human being, not even the proverbial worst enemy. (I should point out this was/is my voice. I don't *hear* voices or have any kind of psychosis.) Day in, day out, I would verbally abuse myself and I know from talking to others with low self-esteem issues it is all too common.

Then imagine being afraid of just about every person who comes across your path. If that's hard to imagine, think how you would feel if people were lions and every day you had to go up to them, speak to them and hear them roar. It may not be rational but the fear inside is just the same. Sometimes you can reassure yourself that their roar is bigger than their bite, but even doing this takes time and effort. And it only takes someone to roar a bit louder than normal, for instance, to bib their hooter at you at a road junction or frown disapprovingly at you in the supermarket queue, and the anxiety tips over into outright fear and panic.

Then there are your imaginings about the future. Not what is happening around you now but about what will happen tomorrow and the day after and the day after that. What if I can't cope with the meeting? What if they are angry with me? What if I make a fool of myself? What if I get ill again? What if I can't work and lose my house? What if I run over a cyclist while driving and get sent to prison?

And while these thoughts are going through my head, because my imagination is so vivid, the emotions that accompany them are as intense as they would be if the experience was already taking place.

And remember, this is not just for a day or two, or a week or a month, but for years and years and years. You can see how it's tempting to give up hope and start thinking about a way out.

These might not be the exact questions and worries your subconscious throws at you on a daily basis, but I'm guessing if you're reading this that you, or someone close to you, knows exactly what I mean. And if you don't, statistics tell us that someone on the bus you took this morning or in the shop that was so busy when you did your food shop on Saturday, or who hid behind the closed doors you drove past on your way home from work is feeling exactly that way right at this minute. As I said in the prologue, we don't all have flashing lights over our heads like self-service tills, but if we did, a good proportion of us would be flashing and silently crying out to be fixed.

Maybe you are in that place right now. Maybe you are living something similar. Because I know these feelings are grim reality, in every town, on every street even, someone will be looking for a way out. The statistics speak for themselves and if I have written this book for one reason only, it is to let you know that you are not alone.

Suicidal behaviour is a complex phenomenon that usually occurs along a continuum, progressing from suicidal thoughts, to planning, to attempting suicide, and finally dying by suicide.

International Association for Suicide Prevention

I have only once made any sort of serious attempt at suicide (and it wasn't really that 'serious'), but having said that, any attempt should be taken seriously. There is no such thing as a 'cry for help'. If someone has gone as far as to plan a way to end their life and then act on that plan then it should never be dismissed lightly.

For that one attempt where I actually followed through my plans there have been thousands of days in my life where I have been holding on by a thread. In my twenties, when I was first diagnosed with depression, for a period of over a year I carried around a bottle of ninety-six aspirin everywhere I went 'just in case' things got too much to cope with. I held off using them by thinking, 'I'll just get through today and then we'll see what tomorrow brings.' Sometimes that wasn't enough and I would take life hour by hour, I would use all my energy and resources on just getting through an hour at a time. At my worst that reduced to fifteen minutes. My life was broken down into fifteen-minute segments: 'Right, I've made it – now for the next fifteen minutes!'

So the fact that I only actually followed through once is a cause for celebration. It also proved to me that behind every attempt that any one person makes there is a whole backdrop of desolation and desperation. Many people around us are battling every day with the thought that they would be better off dead or that the world would be a better place without them. But it's not the sort of thing we talk about – and if we do it's easier to dismiss and say things like 'Don't be so silly' (I too am guilty of this) than to take the time to acknowledge the depths of emotion the person is feeling. Never underestimate the effort it takes for some people just to make it through each day.

It's not just adults, either. More and more in our chaotic and fast-paced society children are feeling suicidal and, in some tragic cases, succeeding in carrying it out. The sad fact is that life is becoming more and more depressing for many of us, even the very young.

> The British Medical Association estimates that at any point in time up to 45,000 young people under the age of 16 are experiencing a severe mental health disorder, and approximately 1.1 million children under the age of 18 would benefit from specialist mental health services.
>
> *Fundamental Facts About Mental Health*,
> Mental Health Foundation, reproduced with kind permission

I can't say I ever thought of suicide as a child but I frequently felt world-weary and believed that the universe was conspiring against me. I wrote the following poem at the age of fourteen, which gives an insight into my gloomy and melancholy outlook on life from an early age.

Why?

What is the reason for life?
There's no hope,

Only dreams
And wherever you go everything seems
Just the same.
From the moment of birth
To the second of death
You're always alone.
For no matter how hard any one of us tries
It's impossible to fathom the unendable size
Of the meaning of life.
Yet through the chaos and tension life still goes on.
There seems no reason
Except maybe one?
The thought that somebody somewhere has found a song
That will light up the heart and bring peace.

'*Why?*' by Gail Marie Lockwood

Receiving the Golden Gate Bridge picture was a turning point but it wasn't an instant fix-all. It would be eighteen months before I could contemplate any sort of employment and more than two years before I could even hope that I had put the worst behind me. In fact, for several months after I had made my felt-tip small-steps plan, even fifteen minutes of life seemed too long to contemplate.

For some reason that I cannot fathom I had decided to have a party for my birthday! I had received a diagnosis of social phobia, I was on strong medication, I had been off work for many months. I didn't like leaving the house, I didn't like being around people. What possessed me to invite twenty people round to celebrate my birthday?!?

Maybe it was one of my many attempts to prove I was still normal. Maybe I was trying to get back to my old self. Certainly it was part of the battle within me against this 'illness', much like the many other times I have stuck my head above the parapet and said, 'I'm not going to let it beat me' only to get shot down in a blaze of ignominy.

Well on that occasion it certainly did beat me. I think I managed half an hour before one of my guests criticised me about a quiz I had prepared. I panicked, freaked out, but as they were all in my house I had nowhere to run. I locked myself in my bedroom and, while my guests were downstairs having a good time, I was shaking, rocking, tearing my hair out and downing a dozen pills.

My lovely friend Kathryn was the only one who noticed I wasn't at the party and I can always remember her slipping a note under the door of my room. I wish I had kept the note and I can't remember what it said exactly, but I knew that she knew what I was going through and I knew she cared. (If only everyone who is at the end of their tether had a Kathryn to slip a note under the door, sometimes that is all it takes to get you through.)

If I'm honest I think the only reason I didn't succeed in taking my own life was that I (thankfully) didn't actually have that many pills to take. I didn't call an ambulance, but I woke up the next morning – feeling terrible but definitely not dead! I had a check-up with the GP, who was well aware of my persistent suicidal thoughts and general mental ill health, but it was a bit late by then for any stomach pumping. You see even as a suicide risk I am an abject failure.

Would I have tried again the next day? Or the next? I guess the moment had passed, but again we will never know. I took the decision to visit my dad in Essex thanks to the offer of a lift from some more good friends who probably didn't want the responsibility of leaving me alone in the state I was in. A few days of rest, a change of scene. It didn't solve my problems or provide a cure but it helped the moment to pass.

Tips from my Toolbox: GPs, Professional Help and Medication

For anyone who is in crisis or who has any concerns whatsoever about their mental health my advice is always go to see your doctor. Do not pass go, do not collect £200, go and get some professional help. I would never deter anyone from seeking help from a qualified medical practitioner. Having said that, it is worth saying that it's not always easy. Plucking up the courage and the motivation to seek help can be an overwhelming task, and the support you get can vary depending on the views and expertise of the GP you see, but in my experience it has always been worth persisting.

Imagine a person, man or woman, who could recite the highway code back to front and upside down. A person who had passed their driving theory test with flying colours and in addition had studied car mechanics and could spot and repair any fault with a little bit of tinkering and elbow grease. Possibly this person could identify hazards on the road ahead and be able to correct other drivers' mistakes with blinding accuracy. Perhaps this person would make an excellent driving instructor, you might be happy to have them teach you or your son or daughter how to drive. Except for one thing: imagine that they had never actually been behind the wheel of a car and had never even started an engine let alone got out of first gear! Would you trust them to guide and advise you, then?

That's possibly a little how I feel about doctors on the subject of mental health. They know all the theory but most of them don't know what it feels like to be hysterical or despairing or suicidal.

No man is a good doctor who has never been sick himself.
Chinese proverb

That's probably asking too much – after all, they don't have Parkinson's disease or sleep apnoea but they know how to treat those who are diagnosed with these illnesses – and for the most part GPs know how to treat mental health issues too. But let's face it, while the best of them can empathise they are never going to actually understand.

Given all that, the absolute first thing I will do when I'm facing a mental health crisis is contact my GP, or out-of-hours doctor if it's the weekend. They are the first people I will call for help because, above most others, they can actually help. They can prescribe medication, they can sign a note that gives a brief interlude from the stresses of work, they can advise on therapies or therapeutic activities. And while bad GPs I would run a mile from do exist, there are many more sensible and understanding ones who will listen and take what is being said seriously.

It can take a great deal of courage for someone who is anxious or depressed to make an appointment and actually turn up to see a doctor. First, you have to make the call. That can leave your heart racing. Then you have to navigate the wrath of the doctor's receptionist: 'What do you want to see the doctor about?' (None of your business); 'Is this really an emergency?' (It is to me – it's the end of the world); 'Can you wait until a week on Thursday?' (I'm not sure I can wait until 5 p.m. this afternoon!). All of which heightens the guilt that there are really sick people out there who more urgently need a doctor and you really shouldn't be bothering the medical professionals with all your petty peccadillos anyway. Then you've got to actually turn up at the surgery and sit in a crowded waiting room with people coughing and grumbling and usually wait long past your allotted appointment time without running away. After which, when you've finally made it and are sitting face-to-face with the GP, you've still got to explain why you are there while a voice in the back of your head is telling you that you are pathetic and feeble and don't deserve any help!

Oh the relief when the GP takes you seriously!... And the feeling of rejection when he or she doesn't.

Several years ago, when I could feel my mental health deteriorating, I visited the GP. I wanted to see a doctor as soon as possible, so I didn't wait the obligatory ten days necessary for an appointment with my own GP. I saw one of the other practice doctors instead. I sat down and poured my heart out about how stressed I was feeling, how I could feel myself tipping down the slippery slope to time off work, hiding indoors, back on benefits. I think I cried. The GP didn't seem to be listening. He had my whole sorry medical history on his computer screen, he could see the medication I was on, but he didn't seem interested in any of that. He looked at me and, without weighing me or getting his stethoscope out he said, 'You do realise you are morbidly obese, don't you?'

I was gutted! I went into the GP's surgery depressed and came out suicidal! I didn't listen as he gave me dietary advice and told me to visit the nurse. My diet was the last thing on my mind. I started the appointment thinking that my life was going down the toilet yet again; I came out with the same conclusion and thinking I was a physical wreck as well!

It's quite common now for the GP to listen to you and say, 'So what would you like me to do?' For me that's fine. I've been on this road my whole adult life and I am acutely self-aware. I know when I need some sedative type of drug, I know when I need a week off work, I know when I'm far beyond GP help and I need to be referred to someone more specialised. Not everyone is as up on the game as me. They go to the doctor's for advice, not more questions. I've had more than one friend tell me that they felt like screaming in response, 'I DON'T KNOW

THAT'S WHY I'VE COME TO SEE YOU!' My best advice if faced with this situation is to ask the GP what the options are and then, if you are in a calm and rational enough frame of mind, to discuss the pros and cons of each option with them. The GP is the expert on what options are out there but you are the expert on you!

Thankfully, for every experience I've had that resembles the above I have met many more practitioners who have been supportive and understanding. Usually now surgeries will have one particular GP who specialises in mental health issues, but even if they don't, find a doctor who takes you seriously and try to stick with them. Not every mental health condition needs medication or therapy, but you and your GP in partnership (if things work well) should be able to find a plan which suits you.

But what of medication? Many frenemies have told me that I should be able to cope without medication; there is still a great stigma attached to taking it, yet if I was on medication for diabetes or high blood pressure nobody would be urging me to ditch my tablets. Why should taking tablets for a chronic mental condition receive a different reaction from people than taking them for a long-term physical illness? I have been on anti-anxiety medication pretty much continually for the past twenty years and in that time I have left seven jobs through anxiety and have steadily taken jobs offering lower pay, fewer hours and less responsibility to try and help me manage my condition. In two jobs, where I worked for very enlightened employers, I had support workers to help me cope with the general challenges of getting to work without panicking, attending meetings and basically carrying out my duties without crying and running away. In addition to that I have spent a cumulative total of three out of those twenty years living on disability benefits, unable to work at all.

Approximately 2 million people of working age in Britain are currently taking psychiatric drugs, most prescribed by their GP.
Fundamental Facts About Mental Health,
Mental Health Foundation, reproduced with kind permission

In addition to that I have had, while being treated with medication, hundreds if not thousands of panic attacks, many in very public places. I have sobbed in so many supermarkets, broken down in high streets, screamed in crowded places, received innumerable funny looks (and also much kindness) from passers-by due to my weeping and wailing. Once I was so afraid of a door-to-door salesman that I screamed the house down with such ferocity that my neighbour came round thinking I was being murdered. On another day a cat got in to my house and I became hysterical. I rang my mum screaming and crying to come and get the cat out of my house even though she lived 150 miles away. I have been close to suicide for months and years of my life. I'm very lucky never to have been sectioned given the number of displays of hysteria I've had. Does that sound like someone for whom medication is working? But then again, what would I have been like without medication?

If medication is the right course of action for you, it is worth persisting to find the correct treatment. I took SSRIs (more info on page 41) for about sixteen years. Four years ago I changed to SNRIs, which have noticeably improved my symptoms. In the future maybe new drugs will come out that will alleviate my anxiety altogether.

For me, I think taking medication is now a life-long thing. If I had diabetes or heart disease I wouldn't worry about taking medication every day, so what is different about mental health issues? However, it isn't necessary for most people to take medication for so long. If you are prescribed medication, don't feel you will be on it forever, but when you do stop taking it make sure you do so slowly, with the support of your doctor.

Nowadays, the National Institute for Health and Care Excellence (NICE) guidelines recommend that GPs offer talking therapies or self-help techniques for mild to moderate anxiety and depression rather than reaching for the prescription book. That would be ideal if it wasn't for the long waiting list and lack of availability of talking therapies. Even to have an assessment over the phone can involve waiting for weeks. At the very least GPs should discuss the side effects and pros and cons of any medication with a patient before starting them on a course of treatment. That's ideal, but it's a lot of ground to cover in a ten-minute appointment; after all, it'll probably take you nine and a half minutes to explain the problem.

One of the dangers with many anti-anxiety meds is the withdrawal symptoms. I started on a drug in the late nineties that was supposed to be a new wonder drug for social anxiety. What wasn't documented then, but is now, are the hideous withdrawal symptoms that users can go through when coming off the meds.

The first time I tried to come off them was after about six years, when the withdrawal effects were only just becoming known. It is now advised to drop your dose very slowly, but I think I did it that time over a period of three weeks. Some symptoms I could have expected. It may have even been the 'real' me that had been masked by the medication, tearfulness, nervous energy, inability to sleep as though I was high on caffeine, feelings of dread and despondency. Other symptoms were just too weird; I felt like I had electric shocks going through my body, I had static inside my head, on my lips and fingertips. I was also irrationally suicidal. I don't mean I felt depressed and wanted to end my life: I mean I was on the top of a car park one day having just been shopping, feeling quite OK with life (apart from all my usual underlying symptoms), and then from nowhere came the thought that I should just drive off the top of the car park. Not to end it all or to give myself some peace but just because I could.

The thought itself shocked me into realising that my withdrawal wasn't working and the GP quickly put me on to another type of medication, but within less than a week it became clear that something was horribly wrong.

Late one night, in yet another panic, I rang my poor dad who lived 150 miles away. I was beside myself; I didn't know what was happening to me. I was hyped up, so high I might have been on some illegal drug. I was hyper-alert, hypersensitive and hysterical. I had to stay with friends that night, I just couldn't be left on my own, and Dad, after what must have been a sleepless night, arrived around seven the next morning. We got an emergency GP appointment and I can still remember pacing up and down the waiting room, crying and trying to scratch my skin off. If I was able to sit down for a few seconds, I just sat there rocking. It must have worried Dad silly to see me like that.

The GP immediately took me off the new meds (I can't remember for the life of me what they were called) and put me back on the original drug, but it was another week before my mania subsided and several more weeks before I was back to 'normal'. Dad stayed with me all that first week. I had some sort of tranquiliser, which I was only allowed once a day. Dad strictly monitored them. All day I paced and cried and rocked. Dad sat with me hour after hour urging me to 'just get through the next five minutes.' I couldn't eat. I couldn't sleep. I couldn't watch TV. I just waited and watched the clock until 4 p.m. when I could be sedated.

No other withdrawal attempt has ever been so dramatic, but I have never managed to do without medication completely. Is that the withdrawal or is this what I'm really like without them? Maybe I will never know.

Meds have never provided a complete cure; however, I have been gainfully employed for seventeen out of the twenty years I've been taking them. Ninety-nine days out of a hundred I can function as a normal human being, despite how I feel inside. I might have alienated many people I once called friends but I still do have a core of wonderful people who have stuck by me through thick and thin. Could I have done any of that without medication? We will never know.

There are also days and weeks that I wouldn't have made it through without diazepam or some other type of sedating medicine. Although highly addictive, at times these meds have been my only possibility of regaining control over my hysteria. I definitely believe that short-term solutions like this have been essential in the medical treatment of my anxiety.

It's worth also remembering, if you have an inherent distrust of the medical profession (and even if you don't), that there are many other 'experts' out there, working in the voluntary sector. The first one which springs to mind (who along with my GP are also on my speed dial) is The Samaritans. They are available 24/7 every single day of the year by phoning 116 123. They will listen and won't judge. OK, they probably won't have any answers, but it is true that talking can just give you that little lift you need to get you through the next few hours. There are many other charities that specialise in different forms of mental ill health and many are staffed by people who have been through it and come out the other side. There are also national charities specialising in mental health. Look on the internet or ask at the library. You really are not alone.

Every six seconds, somebody contacts us. Ten times a minute, we can help someone turn their life around. That's a privilege, and a huge responsibility.

www.samaritans.org

Doctors aren't perfect and they don't have all the answers, but they do their best; they may not have first-hand experience but they have plenty of knowledge and they have access to and information about some of the best tools available. Some, admittedly, aren't the best at empathising with mental health issues, but even the worst of them are getting better with training and changing perceptions and there are some truly wonderful GPs and mental health practitioners out there. In my opinion it is definitely worth persisting.

Over to You: GPs, Professional Help and Medication

- If you are in crisis or feeling that life isn't worth living, get professional help. Do not pass go, do not collect £200; get someone to help you.
- The Samaritans are available 24/7 on 116 123. It is free to call and completely confidential.
- If your GP isn't very helpful, please persist however hopeless it may seem; try again with another doctor. Most surgeries have a GP who specialises in mental health issues, so you can ask to see them.
- Ask for a double appointment – ten minutes isn't long enough to explain the complexities of mental health issues and to explore your options with a GP.
- It might help to write down what you want to say before you go in or to take a family member or friend with you who can better explain your feelings.
- Don't be put off if your GP suggests medication, but make sure the pros and cons are explained and you understand any possible side effects, how long you will be on the treatment and how long it will take to work.

I'm not a GP – or a pharmacist – but here is a very brief guide to the types of medication you might be offered for anxiety or depression. Most of the information is taken from www.nhs.uk where you can find more detailed and up-to-date information on how the drugs work and the possible side effects (plus details of drugs for more specific conditions such as mood stabilisers for bipolar disorder and anti-psychotics to treat psychosis):

Antidepressants (also used to treat several forms of anxiety and post-traumatic stress) usually take ten days to two weeks before they start to work. There are four main types of antidepressant:

- SSRIs (Selective Serotonin Reuptake Inhibitors) are currently the most widely prescribed antidepressants.
- SNRIs (Serotonin-noradrenaline Reuptake Inhibitors) are usually prescribed if SSRIs aren't working.
- NASSAs (Noradrenaline and specific serotonergic antidepressants) are usually prescribed to people who cannot take SSRIs and have similar side effects.
- TCAs (Tricyclic antidepressants) are an older type of antidepressant with more side effects than those listed above and aren't usually prescribed except for patients with severe depression that haven't responded to other treatments; they also might be used for people with OCD or bipolar disorder.

Benzodiazepines provide near instant relief from acute anxiety symptoms. They work as a sedative and the most common to be prescribed is diazepam. They are only used for short periods, typically two to four weeks, because they are addictive.

Remember, this is an illness albeit an invisible one. You have just as much right to medical treatment as anyone with a physical illness.

* * *

That birthday party may have been a rock bottom milestone in my problematic life but it wasn't the end of my belief that suicide offered the final solution. I finally managed to let go of that belief about five years later, in my mid-thirties, during one of the many counselling sessions I have had over the years. The therapist explained that there are three 'Escape Routes' people use when things get too difficult:

- Kill themselves
- Kill someone else
- Go 'mad'

I have never considered or even been tempted to kill someone else, although I do believe I've probably gone 'mad' on more than one occasion! I realised that killing myself had been my escape route of choice for most of my life. The therapist said it was important to mentally 'close' this escape hatch, i.e. make the conscious decision that it was not something I would ever do.

It was a frightening idea! Closing down my only way out? No way! How could I cope? That was my fail-safe backup if things got too much. It was my answer to everything. How could I say it would never happen? What option would I have then if things got too crushingly overbearing? Over weeks of therapy we talked about this, about my fears of living, of coping with the worst that life could throw at me without running away. We gradually and very slowly 'closed' the escape hatch and eventually I internalised the belief that I would never again choose to end my own life.

At the time the decision didn't seem to have much power or weight. It may sound like psychobabble and even then it seemed a rather silly thing to do. Yet gradually I thought about suicide less and less until there were weeks then months when I never thought about my backup plan at all.

So if I've lived so many days on the edge of existence, thinking my life is not worth living, how can I possibly say 'I Love the Life Less Lived'? For a start, I wouldn't have said it then. Not while I was fighting every negative and anxious thought, and while I was attacking myself at every opportunity for my weakness I didn't think I had anything to celebrate at all.

The truth is that now, looking back, I am grateful to my younger self for every single one of those fifteen minutes in which I held on and hoped for a better future. Because since then there have been many more moments that have been full of joy and wonderment and fascination and I would have missed all of that if I'd given up.

At the conclusion of my life my only achievement may well be that 'I saw it through to the end.' I may even have that engraved on my tombstone, but if that is the best that can be said about me at the end it will be worth it. Life threw everything it had at me, and I saw it through. Can any of us really say any more than that?

'If you are going through hell, keep going.'

Winston Churchill

Winston Churchill famously said, 'If you are going through hell, keep going.' It is no secret that he was plagued by depression all his life; he referred to it as his 'black dog'. He knew a thing or two about going through hell, both in his own mind and, with the world in the midst of a bloody world war, in the physical world as well. Yet there are those who believe that he was such a good leader because of his depression, not in spite of it. Whatever the truth, mental illness did not prevent Churchill achieving greatness. Following a nationwide BBC television poll, in 2002 the public voted him the greatest Briton of all time.

Today I find it hard to believe that I took life so lightly for so long. Life is beautiful and wonderful and has so much to offer. Much of what it has to offer is pain, hurt and worry but now I wouldn't miss a second. Oh I still have my moments, but I know they will pass and I don't come close to acting on them. If I could say one thing to anyone and everyone who is in crisis it would be 'just hold on for another minute, then another, then another; this too shall pass.'

'This too shall pass.'

Let me share with you a legend about the wise King Solomon. One day, Solomon decided to teach one of his trusted advisors an important lesson. He called Ben to him and instructed him to find a ring which had magic powers. It had, according to Solomon, the ability to make a happy man sad and a sad man happy.

Ben, wanting to please King Solomon, searched all over the kingdom for this ring but could find it nowhere. On the verge of giving up he walked the streets of one of the poorest parts of Jerusalem and found an impoverished trader setting out his wares on a shabby old carpet.

Ben didn't hold out much hope as he asked the trader if he knew of a ring that could make a sad man happy but at the same time make a happy man sad. The wise man took a plain ring and engraved something on it. When Ben read the message his face broke out in a smile and he hurried back to King Solomon.

King Solomon was surprised when Ben told him he had succeeded in his mission. He had expected him to come back empty handed, as he knew no such ring existed. He took the ring and read the simple inscription on it:

'This too shall pass.'

CHAPTER THREE

One Woman in a Thousand

When you start on the Life Less Lived, in particular when you experience some kind of mental illness, you will lose people from your life. It is a sad but certain fact that there are some people in this world who can't cope with your problems, and equally there are other people who, in your fragile state, you won't be able to cope with. However, through it all certain very special people will shine through all the trials your friendship undergoes and your relationship will be stronger because of it. I absolutely believe that troubles can bring us together in ways that peace and prosperity never can.

> *Laugh, and the world laughs with you;*
> *Weep, and you weep alone.*
> *For the sad old earth must borrow its mirth,*
> *But has trouble enough of its own.*
>
> Extract from *'Solitude'* by Ella Wheeler Wilcox

Straight after that fateful party I talked about in the last chapter I went back to my home town to stay with my dad for some R&R. It became obvious that word of my 'madness' had spread because when I opened the front door to a family friend the expression of horror on his face at the sight of me made me wonder if I'd accidently donned a Frankenstein's mask. At first he was lost for words, then he stuttered, 'You don't look mad!'

I'm not sure who was more embarrassed, him or me.

Looking back it amazes me that I still have a core of a few faithful friends who saw me through my darkest days and didn't run to the hills screaming. It's not easy to be around someone who is anxious or depressed. They drag you down, they are irrational, erratic, emotional – *I* was irrational, erratic, emotional. I was and still am afraid of many people and things. I was too wrapped up in my own fears and failings to have any empathy for the effect I was having on those around me. I was weak and crying out for help and at the same time I had no ear for the cries of others. Who would have wanted me as a friend?

Henri J M Nouwen, in his book *The Inner Voice of Love: A Journey Through Anguish to Freedom* (a book well worth a read for anyone battling with their inner dialogue) talks about how our needs become so overwhelming to those around us they have no choice but to walk away.

In the presence of the people you love, your needs grow and grow, until those people are so overwhelmed by your needs that they are practically forced to leave you for their own survival.

From *The Inner Voice of Love* by Henri Nouwen

Nouwen wrote this book during a time when he was experiencing (and analysing) his own mental health issues; he is open and honest in his reflections, but this truth was one I found particularly hard to swallow for a long time. Surely other people were the problem, not me! How could I be causing people to leave? I was a fragile nothing of a person! A mouse! A slug! How could anyone be affected, negatively or otherwise, by me?

During the two or three years when I was at my lowest I saw no hope of ever returning to employment but my dad bravely broached this subject with me. Actually it was more of a passing comment, something like 'when you get back to work…' etc.

As soon as he mentioned the word 'work' I was struck with panic, fear and terror. It was as if his very words had physically put me back into a crowded office doing a task I didn't understand with colleagues who did nothing but shout at me. I had no concept of how my emotions were affecting my dad but I knew I could never enter the world of work, with all its traps and snares, ever again.

'Don't be silly, Dad. I'd rather die than go back to work,' I snapped at him.

That was the end of the conversation. I meant it too. Everything about straying out of my comfortable cocoon was such anathema to me that even the thought of it got my heart pounding and nausea and bile rising in my throat.

It was only years later, when I was much recovered, that Dad confided the effect my statement had had on him. For someone who worked fifty years of his life with hardly a day off sick, who got up at 5.30 every morning to commute for over an hour to spend the day doing something he merely tolerated as an occupation just to support us, it was impossible for him to understand how the journey to death, whatever that unknown might entail, was preferable to me than a short bus ride to a part-time job.

My dad is a strong person who has stood as close to the edge of the black hole of my despair as it is possible for another person to stand and not run away. If you met him, especially in later years when he was elderly and frail, he would not be what most people would think of as strong. He's not a fighter, he doesn't talk big, he's never been bombastic or extrovert. He is a quiet, ordinary person who, when it really mattered, had the inner courage to stand by another person who was going through perdition and not walk away.

As a young adult I wanted friends who were popular and successful. I wanted to be with the IN crowd. I saw what I perceived as strength in trendy, happy people and thought I could catch something of what they had. When I became ill those 'friends' deserted me and it took me a long time to realise that what I had mistaken for strength was really shallowness. At the time I despised their disloyalty and lack of faith in me, but looking back I wonder that anyone stuck around at all. I have finally realised how difficult it is for other people to be around someone with mental health issues. In hindsight I can see how impossible it is for people who have no experience of mental ill health to understand how or why an intelligent, confident woman can turn into a panicking, wailing mess in a matter of minutes.

And yet, miraculously, there are some amazing people in this world who saw something in me worth hanging around for and had the strength of character to hold out the supportive hand of comradeship to my weary soul. These true friends often came from the most surprising places and had often battled their own inner chaos and confusion. Outwardly they may have had nothing to boast about, but they have been with me in my darkest hours. I value those people almost above life itself; they are angels among us, disguised in weary bodies, weighed down with their own life's worries.

Let me tell you about my friend Kathryn, yes the same Kathryn who stuck the note under my bedroom door while many others were partying away in my living room oblivious to my battle. That was not the first or the last time that Kathryn has been with me through a long dark night of the soul. She is one of the unsung heroines of the world. She doesn't have a great job (she doesn't have any job!), she has never won a medal or climbed a mountain or started a business. She is as ordinary and unremarkable as anyone you are likely to meet, but she came into my life when I was nose-diving to rock bottom and has never left. We get on – not in the way that we have a hundred and one things in common, because quite frankly we don't, but somehow through our differences she understands. She has always been there. She has never judged, never tried to fix me, just offered me the safety of her living room to calm down.

> When we honestly ask ourselves which person in our lives means the most to us, we often find that it is those who, instead of giving advice, solutions or cures, have chosen rather to share our pain and touch our wounds with a warm and tender hand.
> From *Out of Solitude: Three Meditations on the Christian Life* by Henri Nouwen

I can remember many times that Kathryn has been a nurturing and non-threatening presence in my life. Even at my worst, I still felt comfortable sitting with her in her home, maybe because she didn't talk too much, or pry or try to 'cure' me. Or maybe just because she's been through some thorns and brambles herself. One particular incident that brought us together is almost entertaining in its ridiculousness (although it didn't feel like it at the time).

It was Halloween and all the local primary children were going up and down our street trick-or-treating. I get scared when people knock on my door; even now I don't like it if I'm not expecting anyone. I turned the lights out and didn't answer the first knock. Most of the kids were with parents. I could see up and down the road that there were no large gangs of teenagers, just mums, dads and tots having a good time (this was even before I moved to Knowle West where large gangs of teenagers did prowl the streets on 31 October and many other nights of the year as well). I felt inexplicably afraid.

I stayed with the lights out and didn't answer the second knock, or the third. By the fourth knock I wanted to be left alone. Although only about twenty minutes had passed, by the time the fifth group of people rang my doorbell I was becoming hysterical and feeling under siege. I *knew* it was just a bit of harmless fun but in my mind it was as though Genghis Khan and the whole Mongolian army were battering down my defences. I screamed and cried and became a shaking, quivering bundle of jelly.

Pity the poor family who were the seventh group to walk up to my front door. I flung it open and starting crying. 'I can't stand it! Go away! Leave me alone!' I sobbed at the unsuspecting visitors. I still remember that at first they laughed, thinking I was joining in with the game. The children were hardly old enough to go to school and looked more cute than terrorising in their mini witches' costumes. It took them only a few seconds to realise that I was really terrified. I shut the door. I screamed and wailed. I assume they stood there openmouthed for a few seconds before the parents ushered their kids away while trying to explain what was wrong with the crazy woman at number 72.

(As an aside – if you are out trick-or-treating with your children – please don't knock on the doors of strangers' houses – you really don't know what goes on behind closed doors or who or what might be waiting on the other side.)

I felt sick and fragile and at my wits' end. Embarrassed by my outburst but terrified all the same. Yet again I am at a loss to explain the all-consuming panic that had taken hold of me, panic that I could not control and I believed with all my heart would never end. Enemies were at my door with weapons of mental destruction. I couldn't escape. I didn't know what to do.

So I rang Kathryn. I must have sounded ridiculous! 'The trick-or-treaters are scaring me please come and save me!'

She didn't laugh, she didn't tell me to pull myself together or to snap out of it. She didn't try to rationalise anything. She just strapped her own kids into their pushchair and trotted round to my house.

I used to think that a true friend was one who would come out at 3 a.m. if you called them with an emergency. Now I think a friend is someone who will come out at teatime when she is in the middle of putting the kids to bed, even when all that is wrong is an irrational fear of five-year-olds.

One man in a thousand, Solomon says.
Will stick more close than a brother.
And it's worthwhile seeking him half your days
If you find him before the other.

Nine hundred and ninety-nine depend
On what the world sees in you,
But the Thousandth Man will stand your friend
With the whole round world agin you.
    Extract from 'The Thousandth Man' by Rudyard Kipling

Tips from my Toolbox: Let them people go

It's hard to know how to befriend someone with mental health issues, so how do some people, like Kathryn, seem to do it naturally? What you need when you are low or in crisis is someone who will accept what you are experiencing without judging, who will encourage you to recovery without being bossy and bullying. You need someone who will empathise without revelling in your woes, but most of all, more than any of these things, you need someone who will stick around when the going gets tough even if they don't have a Scooby-Doo what is going on inside your head (because let's face it – you probably don't have a clue either)!

I had a friend once ... let's call her Jenny. We were friends all through university. We shared essay deadline worries and hangovers induced by cider-and-black. We lived in the same residential block, saw each other every day, revised together, partied together and then, when our uni days were done and we had settled into grown-up jobs with adult mortgages we continued our friendship.

Ten years of friendship later she came to stay with me when I was starting my downward spiral. It was shortly before I met Kathryn, around the time I gave up my accountancy job and maybe a couple of years before I had hit the rock bottom of hiding away with only a packet of paracetamol for company. I was maybe manic, maybe anxious, tearful and fraught. I wasn't fun. She'd signed up for a weekend of frolics with her fun-loving uni buddy. She hadn't signed up for a front-row seat into the revealing of my inner pain. This was still the early days of my mental health journey, but I had changed and Jenny hadn't.

I remember sobbing that weekend, I don't remember why. Jenny told me, quite kindly, if truth be told, that she wasn't having a very good weekend with me bawling all the time and she thought she would go home. Which she did and I never saw her again.

For a while I felt a sense of grief and guilt for Jenny. I had certainly failed as a hostess for the weekend and I was pretty sure I had failed as a friend.

Jenny was one of the first to walk out of my life but many more would follow. I used to feel anger at people who've left in this way. Or I would turn the anger on myself at my own failure to maintain relationships. What is wrong with them?! What is wrong with me?! This was particularly in work situations where the law is supposed to protect people with disabilities including invisible ones like anxiety and depression. Inside the paranoia of my mind the 'Jennys' of my life became 'they' and 'they' soon became 'everyone'. Jenny thinks I'm mad. They think I'm mad. Everyone thinks I'm mad.

If there is one tool that has been a more bitter pill than most is to accept how impossible it is for people who have no experience of mental ill health to understand how I can flip from confident to inconsolable in the space of a heartbeat. Accepting the need to move on from such people has been important for my own sanity and peace of mind. Burning with anger and resentment just fuels my own anxiety, depression and self-loathing. Even now I don't always manage this, believe me I don't, but I really work hard to forgive and forget the ones that got away. No one is all evil or all good, each of us is a fluctuating shade of grey. I now realise that they are not bad people they just don't understand, and maybe they have their own battles to fight on a daily basis. Battles of which I am unaware and which mean they don't have the spare reserves to take on my burdens too.

'You wouldn't worry so much about what others think of you if you realised how seldom they do.'

Eleanor Roosevelt

Besides, I doubt Jenny has given me a second thought in the years since our last weekend together. If I am tempted ever to dwell on what I imagine everyone thinks of me I remember the reassuring and humbling words of Eleanor Roosevelt: 'You wouldn't worry so much about what others think of you if you realised how seldom they do.'

At the other end of the scale, as someone with a diagnosis of social phobia, there are as many people who I have ceased contact with as them with me, not because they couldn't cope with me but because I couldn't cope with them. I wouldn't exactly call this a choice, more a survival technique. There is a fallacy in modern society that we need people, but sometimes what we need is solitude. There is a whole world of difference between loneliness and solitude. Loneliness can persist amid the largest crowd but solitude is freedom from the constraints of polite society, liberation from the fripperies of small talk and a relief from the constant demands of others.

> 'The best thinking has been done in solitude, the worst in turmoil.'
>
> Thomas Edison

What's more, other people can be draining, which is all part of the give and take of life when you are on top of things, but if you yourself are feeling fragile and broken it is hard to abide the idiosyncrasies of others. There is a definite need when you are unwell to beware the wolves in sheep's clothing.

When you are vulnerable there are some people who will present themselves to you as companions, advisors and confidantes, when really all they want to do is feed off your insecurities and misery. These people tend to be passive-aggressive individuals who have huge issues of their own but are in denial about it. Take Mark, a friend of mine who was going through a tough time after two close family bereavements. He was pleasantly surprised to find that his 'friend' Andrew was happy to listen and lend a shoulder to cry on. It didn't take long for Mark to realise that he felt much worse after an afternoon in the pub with Andrew; it took him quite a while to realise why. Andrew would listen carefully and then, subtly, twist the knife: 'Well at least I've never been through that,' 'Things come in threes – I wonder who will die next?,' 'I bet you feel really miserable, don't you?,' 'That's just how I felt when I went through this…,' 'You've done nothing with your life… at least I've done…' Andrew loved to relive all the gory details of Mark's misery, which maybe for a while was OK with Mark, but then he wanted to climb out of the 'Slough of Despond' (as described by John Bunyan in *Pilgrim's Progress*). He wanted to move on. Andrew had never moved on from his own problems. He wanted someone who was weaker and more depressed than himself who he could put down for the sole purpose of making himself feel better.

I have one thing to say if you know an Andrew: walk away. Walk away now! Don't feel guilty; don't look back. Run! You are far too precious to be dragged down by the Andrews of this world. Maybe one day they will realise why they are sitting alone in a pub talking to themselves and you can rekindle whatever was good in your friendship, but for the time being just walk away.

Possibly the most common type of person you find yourself coping with when you are down and out are the ones who, for all the best intentions, want to 'fix' you. Usually those closest to you, those most affected by each nuance of your highs and lows. It's amazing how many people suddenly know what is best for you, and how, because you are perceived as weak and ineffectual, your opinion seems no longer to matter. You have no voice. In many ways I was able to escape the influence of the 'fixers' having lived alone for most of my adult life. It's much easier to lock yourself away than to constantly battle to explain what 'the problem is' to someone who is trying hard to understand but quite clearly is never going to be able to.

The long and the short of it is – people are human. It took me years to realise that people are never as good as you need them to be, but that doesn't make them bad. It might, however, make them difficult to cope with when you are using all your energy to cope with yourself. It took me even longer to realise that I am not as good as people need me to be, that I am difficult to cope with – even now, and certainly when I was at the bottom of my pit of angst and despair – but that does not make me a bad person. It does not even make me a weak person. It just makes me human – like the rest of us.

Over to You: Let them people go

- If you have even one person in your life who accepts you for who you are and will sit by you in your darkest hour, you are luckier than you know. They are a treasure worth more than any diamond. Hold on to them.
- Not everyone can cope with your problems. That doesn't make them bad, and it doesn't make you bad, but, for the time being at least, you might have to give them the space they need.
- When you are vulnerable, you may not be able to cope with certain people (or indeed **any** people). That doesn't make you a bad person, it doesn't make them bad people. It's OK to take the time and space you need to heal yourself.

* * *

Some time after receiving my Golden Gate picture from my mum, early on during the road to recovery, I remember another small but pivotal moment. A simple memory but one that still comes back to me now at crucial times when I need that little bit of extra strength to get through the day. It also shows how, even people we don't know and may even have never met can have a profound influence on our lives.

Some people make music because they want to become rich and famous; you see them on TV talent shows every Saturday night, and many of these people produce songs that get your feet tapping and lift your emotions. For me I have always been drawn to the musicians who travel off the beaten track because generally these are the ones who use music because they have something in their soul that they want to communicate with the world. It's not (to quote Jessie J) about the money, money, money. There is one musician who has saved my life on more than one occasion (and I quite honestly mean he has saved my life), whose music has influenced and encouraged me for the past two decades – I'm putting money on the fact that you'll never have heard of him.

Martyn Joseph is a Welsh singer-songwriter who performs around two hundred live shows a year all around the UK, Europe and North America. He was once signed to Sony Records. He once got to number 34 in the charts. He has toured with many artists over his career and was briefly the supporting act for Shirley Bassey. Every night Bassey fans turned up to see her in sequins and hear 'Hey Big Spender'. To warm them up Martyn came on in jeans and a T-shirt and sang about redundant Welsh miners. Suffice to say the two didn't mix and Shirley and Martyn parted company after just ten shows. True, Martyn could have smartened up his act, pulled a few upbeat love songs out of the bag and gone on to bigger and greater things, but that's not what he is about, and I for one am glad.

There are numerous Martyn moments that have spoken to my soul. I was introduced to him in my rock bottom years and I immediately felt that there was someone here who understood my dilemmas and was able to express the mysteries of life in lyrical form. Martyn has often said that writing songs is therapy for him. Listening to his music is certainly therapy for me. The very first song of his that I heard was 'Treasure the Questions'. In a world that is always trying to provide us with answers I was struck by the idea that we don't need to have everything all worked out. In fact those people who do have all the answers are often the most shallow and arrogant. Life is too complex and intricate to fully understand.

One evening, somewhere on my slow road to recovery after receiving the Golden Gate Bridge picture, I heard that Martyn was playing in Cardiff. I was living in Bristol at the time. It was a long drive and I was no way confident enough to go to a concert on my own, but then again I'd alienated most of my friends and didn't have anyone to take me. I very nearly didn't go but something inside made me take the hour-long trip to a tiny little venue in Cardiff Bay. Maybe it was the chance to tick off another 'small step' on my road to recovery. I sat at the back feeling like I always felt in those days: worthless, useless, nothing.

Martyn came on and his songs began to thaw my icy void of negative emotions. I began to open up to the possibility that there might be other ways of looking at things. Maybe there was more to me than a weak, pathetic failure. Then came a moment of clarity that I will never forget when Martyn sang a cover version of U2's 'Stuck in a Moment You Can't Get Out Of'. I cried and cried as I listened to the lyrics. If anyone was stuck in a moment, it was me! It was a long moment – it had lasted years rather than seconds and I certainly was having trouble getting out of it. I had heard the song many times before, but somehow hearing Martyn sing it in that small venue I felt as though the words were written for me. I went home, bought the CD and wrote down all the lyrics. I turned a small corner. True, I had many more corners to turn, but we get where we are going by turning small corners and taking tiny steps, not with great leaps and instant makeovers.

In his book *Notes on Words*, Martyn talks about his motivation to write and perform his music. His aim is to 'walk out there, bridge that gap and drag you somewhere a little better than the place you were before you came through the door, and give you a better view.' Martyn does that for me every time, and reading comments by countless other people on his website and on social media, it's obvious he does it for many other people too. If he's ever in your local town I urge you to pay him a visit. You won't be disappointed.

Friends drop by say you'll be OK
Loving glances and they walk away
Now you're wearing that volunteer smile
But it's not how you feel and it's not what's inside you
And it feels like this…
When you can't see the end
Hey I understand
When it feels like this.

Extract from *'Feels Like This'*, by Martyn Joseph
Reproduced with kind permission

All these years on, Martyn is still my favourite artist. I still go to his gigs whenever he is playing locally. He still turns up on stage looking like he's just got off the sofa after a long nap. He still sings songs about rebellion and justice, heaven and earth. He wouldn't look out of place with his guitar under the railway arches at Charing Cross Station but when he sings – oh when he sings! – it's like a little window opens between here and paradise and you can overhear a conversation between angels!

Tips from my Toolbox: Music

I don't have a musical bone in my body – despite thousands of piano lessons and exams as both an eager child and a recalcitrant teen, I was only able to learn to read music by sheer determination. I could never 'hear' the music I was playing. The notes came out in more or less the correct order and I allegro-ed when it said allegro and crescendo-ed as I was instructed to do so, but nothing ever came naturally. I couldn't sing a note – worse than that, people laugh and cover their ears when I sing. Even my closest family, who patiently endure the worst of my habits and foibles, cringe when I sing along to the radio. I once had a whole auditorium of around a thousand people creased up in tears of laughter as I attempted to warble a short ditty (one of the worst moments of my life!!).

Music as a tool for therapy is not the sole domain of the Mozarts and Lennons of this world. Even I, tone-deaf and unmelodious as I am, have gained important wisdom and insights from music. I may not understand the key changes and the harmony lines, I might be unable to detect a saxophone from a violin and I don't know my riff from my roll, but somehow music has the ability to communicate at all levels of appreciation and ability. It's almost mystical the power music has over a person's mood. Songs can put a smile on our faces, make us cry, bring a stillness or a sadness. Lyrics can give a sense that someone has walked your path before you, they can give you hope or at least bring the realisation that someone empathises with your hopelessness. They can speak to our soul. Singing together can bring a sense of community; whether it be in a church or a football stadium, music brings people together in a way that very little else I can think of has the power to do.

In 2014, BBC Radio Two's Faith in the World week focused on the healing power of music. They conducted a poll to find the top ten songs to listen to when feeling down. In the survey, 81 per cent of people polled said listening to music made them feel better. The week focused on a 'powerful range of stories from those with mental ill health, sensory loss or motor neurone disease to American war veterans and those in need of comfort and healing. All have found certain songs and rhythms have had a profound effect on them.'

The week also gave attention to music therapy, which is used by professionals to support a range of people from children to adults with learning difficulties to those with dementia (www.bamt.org).

Needless to say, you don't need to go and see a professional to experience the benefits that music can bring. Everyone knows how music can make you feel. So my tip is this: Use music to your advantage in controlling your moods. That isn't to say only ever listen to happy music – there are times when we need to be thoughtful, or sad, or uplifted – but I have found it very useful to be aware of how I need to feel and to use music to help me get to where I need to be.

This is easier than ever in an age of MP3 players. I have created several playlists for different times and moods. It is tempting to give you my playlists, song by song, but the tunes that make me smile are not necessarily the same ones that will work for you. Besides, my lists are fluid and change from month to month. Suffice to say my cheerful tunes contain numerous upbeat, boppy tunes, for example, 'Happy' by Pharrell Williams, 'Chelsea Dagger' by The Fratellis and old classics like 'I Love to Boogie' by T. Rex.

I also have a 'strong songs' playlist for times when I need to face something which I feel I can't cope with filled with inspirational tunes such as '(Something Inside) So Strong' by Labi Siffre and 'I Am Woman' by Helen Reddy. Then there is my 'thoughtful playlist' if I just want to think about life, the universe and everything in between, which contains little known gems like 'Crossroads' by Don McLean and 'That'll Do' by Kenny Loggins. I also frequently feel the need to listen to calming music, usually classical, when I feel anxiety approaching but am able to notice it in time to restrain it.

Music is like time travel, hearing a song can instantly transport us back to a memory, bring long forgotten friends to the forefront of our minds but, more than anything else, music has the power to heal, it can somehow reach the places in our soul that words or medicines can't find.

Over to You: Music

- Over the next few days pay attention to how different music can alter your mood.

- Sort through your CDs, vinyls or MP3 and prepare your list of songs for different moods. Do it now, before you need them, and they will be there as a tool when you hit rock bottom.

* * *

How did I get through the two years that followed me receiving my Golden Gate Bridge challenge? It would make a fantastic story if I could give you a simple three-step how-to guide that you could follow and we could all be rid of our fears and failings. It didn't work like that; it was more of a stumbling in the dark than a light switching on. I had limited tools consisting of medication, a small step plan to success (which was very amateurish and slightly pathetic), some inspiring music, a good friend and a family who cared even if they couldn't understand. It wasn't much to go on and it amazes me that I got through it at all.

I've told you a few key moments, but there were many more 'nothing' moments. Many days and nights I lay in bed crying. Countless panic attacks which spun me back to square one. Many friends left me and I cried bitter tears of regret over their loss. I cut myself off from many other people who, I felt, were dragging me down, and I cried more bitter tears of guilt over my inability to cope.

No, looking back, the best thing I can say about that time is that I held on.

I held on through the nothing days. I held on through the suicidal days. I held on through each new panic attack. I held on through disappointment and despair. I held on.

On any day where I felt a little positivity, I would look at my small steps and my Golden Gate Bridge picture and I would make a gargantuan effort to do something which moved my plan forward. At first those days were rare – but they were healing. Exhausting but healing. After a time the gap between the good days became smaller. The downward spirals didn't dip so deep. Gradually and oh-so slowly the good days began to outnumber the bad days.

I say this not to discourage you but to let you know (if you are hiding under a duvet) that the nothing days are OK. I still have nothing days and I still feel a little guilty! Yet I know they are necessary in order to rest and recuperate.

I say this to let you know (if you were doing really well and have just had another panic attack) that setbacks are OK. They are all part of the recovery process. You will never go back to square one because you are stronger now and have learned lessons along the way.

I say this also because it is easy to read a few pages and believe that I had some sort of miracle cure and for you to feel a failure because the same hasn't happened to you. There was no miracle cure. I wasn't strong. I didn't immediately turn my life around. There isn't enough paper and ink in the world to tell you all about my disappointments, failings and embarrassments during those two years. It was slow and painful, but I now realise that was all part of the process.

Not that I didn't want an instant cure. I desperately wanted to be better and pick up my life exactly where it had left off. I focused on reaching the Golden Gate Bridge as a symbol that I was back to my old self. I will forever be grateful for that picture and that goal, but it was a shallow goal. Of course travelling halfway across the world would be a huge achievement for someone afraid to go to Tesco, but what I never realised until much later was that there were deeper, wider aims that I needed to be aiming for. Things like accepting myself as a whole person with frailties and imperfections; having the strength to build a lasting relationship; finding a job which I found fulfilling and didn't run away from; discovering who I was and liking myself and my place in the world; being gentle with my anxiety and depression instead of battling them.

I now realise that the Golden Gate Bridge was simply a stopping point on a longer and more interesting journey. At the time I could only see the next stopping point because I couldn't even begin to envisage the steep mountains and desolate moors which were to follow. My myopia was a blessing; if I could have foretold what was to come in the next few years I may well have stayed where I was and refused to take another step! If I had done that I would have missed out on an amazing journey, wonderful travelling companions and experiences that gave me strength and wisdom and also many smiles and laughter. At that point I didn't need to know the whole journey, none of us do. I didn't need the strength to cope with everything that was to follow; I just needed to take the next step.

CHAPTER FOUR

Look Ma, No Hands

Less than two years after I received the Golden Gate Bridge photo I was standing in front of an armed cop at the immigration desk at JFK airport waiting to be let into the United States of America. Totally alone, I had flown 3500 miles, but the hardest part had been getting to the stage where I could even get on the plane. Standing there, vulnerable and faced with the enormity of what I was doing, I truly thought I was out of my mind.

'State the purpose of your visit,' the cop ordered, in a stern New York accent.

'Umm, I'm travelling around America – for, er, a holiday, for ten weeks,' I stuttered, convinced I looked and sounded guilty and was about to be arrested.

The cop frowned; he had big bushy eyebrows and a seventies moustache. I sweated. I was tired. I'd flown for eight hours, queued for what seemed like another eight, I still had to find a way into New York City and find my hotel. I was very, very scared.

'Who are you travelling with?'

'Er, um, I'm travelling on my own.'

He looked up at me for the first time with incredulity. We were both aware that I didn't look like a seasoned traveller. I decided he thought I was an idiot – or worse – a liar. He was going to refuse me entry!

He looked down at my papers again and typed something into the computer. I fretted and worried – imagining all sorts of scenarios involving arrest, imprisonment and a trip to Guantanamo Bay! Finally, much to my relief, he stamped my passport.

'You go, girl!' he said with a smile of admiration (and in a way only a gruff cop from New York could get away with)!

He was impressed! He thought I was brave and confident to be travelling alone around America. He thought I rocked! He didn't actually say any of that – I'm reading between the lines here, but he obviously thought it impressive that I was making this journey. He didn't know the half of it! He had no idea how far I'd come to get here. I felt a little surge of pride…

…Then a huge surge of fear. I still had several weeks and many miles to get to the Golden Gate Bridge and all of a sudden my family and friends seemed far, far away. If I'm honest it was far too soon to be tackling such a ridiculously huge trial; this was no 'small step', but I was determined to prove that my anxious days were behind me, determined to embrace life and make up for the years I'd lost sitting around hiding behind my front door in panic. In truth, I was probably in denial. I was convinced I was 'cured' and unwilling to accept the fundamental part of my psyche that houses the anxiety, fear and depression. I was fighting with myself instead of accepting myself. Not the best plan but it had got me Stateside. Things could've been a lot worse.

Unfortunately, my anxious days were far from behind me. Within three weeks I would be sitting behind another door, far from home and quaking with fear, my dream of reaching the Golden Gate Bridge looking like an absurd and unattainable illusion.

I was to travel around America with an organised tour, which would take us down the east coast as far as the Florida Keys, back up through Alabama and Louisiana and into Texas, before doing the main tourist spots of the Grand Canyon, Las Vegas and finally moving on to California. San Francisco was five weeks away. After this highlight the tour would continue up the west coast of the USA, into Canada, and across the northern states of the US until we returned to New York ten weeks later. It had looked fantastic in the brochure, and was 'cheap' because we were camping ninety per cent of the time, cooking our own food and travelling on a rather small minibus that was quite a squash, especially on the numerous days we travelled for ten or twelve hours straight.

Needless to say, by this time I was slightly less anxious than I had been in the preceding years. I had knocked my social phobia into submission by repeatedly pushing myself out of my comfort zone and I'd had some lucky breaks. For one, I'd managed to get a job working for an organisation which promoted the rights of disabled people and they were happy to take on someone with ongoing mental health issues. This doesn't happen to everyone (and it certainly doesn't always happen to me!), but they were able to arrange funding for a support worker who helped me with the tasks at work I found difficult – like interacting with people! Going to work, even part-time, was hard, but it did increase my confidence. I also made the decision to move from Bristol back to my home town of Nottingham. Maybe this was an upheaval I could ill afford at such a vulnerable stage in my life but it gave me a sense of progress, of moving on, of getting where I wanted to go (and leaving behind the scene of my demise).

In the middle of all that I headed off on my Great American Adventure to prove to the world and his wife (and my mum) that I was better and I could achieve my dream. There may have been good argument for procrastinating, for waiting a couple of years, for giving myself time to get stronger. I didn't know it then, but time wasn't on our side if I wanted my mum to stare proudly at a picture of me by the Golden Gate Bridge and boast to her friends that I'd made it.

* * *

Three days after arriving at JFK I met the rest of my travelling companions. I sat on the bus feeling stupidly shy, but then I guess that's how most people would feel. There were twelve of us in total, including the tour leader, most of us British and everyone much younger than myself – several of them not even old enough to legally drink in the US!

Camp life was liberating but also very claustrophobic. I shared a very small two-person tent with a girl from the UK who I had never met before. The twelve of us cooked together, showered together (not literally; we had our own cubicles), travelled together, packed and unpacked the tents and luggage together. For someone who had lived alone for ten years and not only valued her privacy but had been diagnosed with social phobia it was a challenge, but we were on the open road and, looking out of the van watching mile after mile of US freeway flying by, I felt a sense of my life being back on the right track.

For the first two weeks life was bliss. I quickly adapted and we all got on well. We had so many laughs and adventures on that trip, I could write a whole novel about it (but that's for another time). We danced in fountains in Charleston, watched the sunset from beaches on the Florida Keys and learned about each other and our lives. We snorkelled, met the friendliest Americans you could ever imagine and drank cocktails (those of us who were old enough anyway) at Jimmy Buffett's Margaritaville – where the clock always says 5 p.m.

Looking back I remember the high points in far more detail than I remember the low points; the human memory is kind that way. But there were low points to follow – Charles Dickens could have been writing about my trip when he said 'It was the best of times, it was the worst of times.' As I sat drinking a margarita, laughing with my new friends and feeling on top of the world, I never guessed that the 'worst of times' were just a few days away.

It was the best of times, it was the worst of times.
From *A Tale of Two Cities* by Charles Dickens

I woke the day after Jimmy Buffett's with a really sore throat and glands the size of golf balls. Time had moved on, the 'it's always 5 o'clock at Margaritaville' was as much of a myth as my positive mental state. For as long as I can remember I cry when I'm tired and I cry when I'm ill. After three weeks the late nights exploring the bright lights and the early mornings packing up tents and travelling hundreds of miles had caught up with me. I was tired, ill, dirty, hot, mosquito bitten and far from home, which called for big tears. I had my first major homesick moment on the alligator tour of the Everglades. I was so miserable and fed up and kept crying like an idiot. I wanted my friends around me not a bunch of strangers and I wanted to really get away and be on my own.

Unfortunately, there were alligators all around the boat, so there wasn't that far I could go. My travelling companions were brilliant; I wasn't the first one to be homesick, or the first one to cry. The trouble with me is keeping these things in perspective.

It was so hard being around people ALL THE TIME. Mostly they were good friendly people, which made it easier, but I needed my own space, I needed to have a bath and keep clean. I needed to be able to wear clothes that weren't dirty and creased. I needed a day of rest. I didn't have the youth or the mental resilience of my travelling companions and once the 'nasty gnomes' had started telling me of all my failings it was difficult to shut them up:

'You're too old for this'
'What were you thinking travelling on your own'
'No one likes you'
'You will fail at this just like you fail at everything else'
'You are a crazy mental person – you should be locked up'

In my exhausted state it was easy to believe and dwell on these negative thoughts and at that time I had no real training or experience that would help me challenge them.

It is easy to ask why I didn't just snap out of it. I wonder that often as I reflect all these years later. I know I told myself to pull myself together then. I was in one of the most beautiful places on earth on the adventure of a lifetime. But mental health doesn't work like that; it knows no reason or logic. Despair and panic can strike at the most unlikely and inconvenient times and yet keep quiet when we're going through real trials. If only it were that easy to overcome inner demons, then my life would have turned out very differently. Unfortunately, my negativity began to spiral out of control and events were going to get far worse.

Tips from my Toolbox: Eat, Move, Sleep

Nowadays, I believe in a holistic approach to mind and body. Anxiety and depression aren't just mental issues – they produce real physical symptoms: headaches, digestive problems, tension, nausea, insomnia, heartburn, migraines and lethargy, to name a few. Likewise, if you are in constant pain or have a physical illness you are more than likely going to feel down. Keeping my body as healthy as can be doesn't come naturally. I'm not at all fit, I don't enjoy exercise and I love chips and takeaways! It has taken me a long time to learn that when my body feels healthy I am better able to cope with any swings in my mood. It has taken me even longer to respect the physical needs of my body and not expect it to defy science.

In America I expected my body to cope with late nights and early mornings, I fed it junk food and alcohol, I sat in a bus for hours straight and did very little exercise. Some people have reserves of stamina and strength that I don't have. On my US journey I refused to acknowledge that I had physical needs which needed to be met. That I was weaker than my younger travelling companions, that I needed to nourish, refresh and rest my body. If I'd taken more physical care of myself things may have worked out better. I'd like to say I learned the lesson then. Sadly not. I'm still learning now even though I know for a fact that it is vitally important to Eat, Move and Sleep.

Eat

I'm a big girl. I'm big boned. No, let's face it: I'm fat! A fact which does not help my anxiety and depression one bit. This tip is a case of 'do as I say, not as I do.' Having said that I do try. I know that eating a healthy diet will aid my mental health, but as soon as something goes wrong I reach for a high-fat, high-sugar processed snack. Maybe I shouldn't berate myself too much for this; after all, who really thinks 'I'm really stressed I just fancy an apple!'?

Losing weight is hard at the best of times. It goes against every animal instinct we have. Our ancestors needed to eat when they could and store fat because they never knew when they would find food again. Meals in days of yore meant catching or growing it, building a fire, preparing it, waiting for it to cook for several hours and then eating. Nowadays, we can roll up at a drive-through at any time of day or night or pick up any number of microwavable concoctions at a supermarket that's open 24/7.

You are what you eat, so don't be fast, cheap, easy or fake.
Fridge magnet

I don't need to tell you how to eat healthily for mind and body. You already know! More fruit and vegetables and fewer cakes and crisps; more fresh ingredients and fewer processed meals. Plenty of water, not so much fizzy pop. Eat when you are hungry and stop when you are full. It's simple! However, there is a whole industry of food/diet marketing executives who try and bamboozle us with facts, figures and advertising claims. Oh and you have to keep at it, day after day after month after year! I feel so good if I've eaten healthily for a day – only to realise I have to do it all again tomorrow! A couple of friends were recently referred by their GP to a well-known slimming club. They did really well. They lost several stone between them in six weeks. Fantastic! But they were only referred for six weeks, so after that they, of course, put all the weight back on. Wouldn't any of us?

A couple of years ago I joined a local healthy-eating club. It was started by a qualified dietician and a life coach/hypnotherapist. Between them they knew everything possible about making healthy permanent lifestyle changes that would lead to long-lasting improved health and slow but steady weight loss.

It was the BEST club of its kind, far better than any of the major national groups that I have tried before. It gave intelligent, well-researched dietary information and excellent tools for changing habits. It advocated fresh natural foods with occasional treats but nothing faddy. Eating protein at every meal, a diet low in refined sugar but with plenty of oily fish, nuts and seeds. No counting, no expensive diet foods or shakes to purchase; they even researched local supermarkets to see where you could get ingredients and foodstuffs more cheaply. While the dietician gave advice on portion control and nutritious healthy meal planning the life coach gave us tools on the difficult bit… how to avoid temptation. We explored the reasons we stress eat and comfort eat, how to balance our blood sugars to avoid cravings, making small and lasting changes rather than drastic detoxing, visualisation of our goals and celebrations of our achievements.

It was perfect! I loved it!

It never caught on!

After eighteen months it closed through lack of interest (but I should quickly say not through lack of success for those of us who attended!). Maybe they outdid themselves, because people learned good habits, lost weight and didn't need to go back. I don't know – I do know that small healthy changes and taking a long-term lifelong approach are the only things that really work to improve health and fitness.

And yet unhealthy food is so tempting! So I try to eat well when I am mentally well, in the hope that it will prepare me for any future crisis. I minimise foods that I know mess with my head (namely alcohol and sugar) because I know these can alter my mood quite dramatically and immediately. I try to resist comfort foods when I am low but I no longer give myself a hard time if I do slip up. Life is difficult enough and sometimes, in spite of all the evidence to the contrary, a tray of chips and melted cheese really is the best medicine.

Over to You: Eat Well

- Make small lasting changes to your diet, for example:
  - More fruit and vegetables, fewer cakes and crisps.
  - Eat protein at every meal to avoid hunger pangs.

- More healthy fats from seeds, nuts and oily fish, and less saturated fat from chips and burgers.
  - Reduce your refined sugar intake (from cakes, sweets, fizzy drinks) to balance your blood sugar levels and avoid cravings and mood swings.
  - More complex carbohydrates (wholegrain bread, rice, beans) and fewer simple carbohydrates (white bread, cakes, sugar).
  - More fresh ingredients, fewer processed meals.
  - More water, less fizzy pop.
  - More sit-down nutritious meals, fewer snacks on the go.
- Don't take on all the above changes in one go! Pick one or two a week and stick to them.
- Avoid draconian diet regimes which make you feel tired and depressed and guilty when you inevitably give up on them. If a way of eating isn't healing your mental as well as physical wellbeing it isn't right for you.
- Avoid labelling any food as 'bad' and never punish yourself for eating something you later regret. Just move on. Tomorrow is a new day.

Move

I am not a sporty person. I have never been a sporty person, never will be. However, the dreaded 'exercise' is supposed to be so good for mind and body. There is even actual scientific proof of it! Over the years I have forced myself to join gyms, bounce around in aerobics classes; I have sweated in unladylike places and strained muscles I didn't even know I had – all in the name of good health. I was even given a 'prescription' for exercise once from my doctor (that wasn't so bad; at least the gym they sent me to was cheap and they understood my limitations). The problem is I hate/detest/loathe exercise with a passion. To me it is bad medicine! More to the point, I always give up after a few days or weeks. 'How can this physical torture be good for me?' I reason – then sneak off to the drive-through with a renewed sense of guilt and failure.

My most intense foray into the world of fitness lasted a couple of years. I discovered Nordic walking (which I still consider a great activity) and took two or three classes a week. Not cheap on my salary but 'it was doing me good' physically at least. I then took up orienteering, which again I enjoyed at the beginning. I signed up with a personal trainer and even took to jogging!!! (Briefly, until I did my back in – morbidly obese people are not designed to jog!)

It all sounds good, doesn't it? I was exercising five or six times a week, and physically there must have been some benefit, although I never lost any weight. Mentally it was draining, futile and frustrating. First, there was the time it took up – together with travelling to and from classes and events it felt like an added pressure and burden that I didn't need in my life. Exercise is supposed to give you energy but I felt exhausted! Even more exhausted than I normally do!

Maybe we make time for the things we enjoy, especially those that are good for us, but was I really enjoying this? Not if the number of times I came home crying was anything to go by. You see I just couldn't keep up! Not surprising in the orienteering group, which was full of teenage boys who could sprint between the markers with ease – I could allow for the fact that everyone was younger and fitter than me but it still felt like I was holding everyone back and being pitied. 'Ah, bless her chubby little legs, at least she's having a go' was what I imagined they were saying. The Nordic walking class was more humiliating – it mostly consisted of people in their fifties and sixties who sped up hills like robots possessed, leaving me huffing, puffing and trailing behind. I spent every hour staring at the back of a rapidly disappearing group of senior citizens. Once or twice I completely lost sight of them and, not being able to figure out which way they had gone, I gave up and made my way home. I don't think anyone noticed my absence. I cursed myself over and over for paying money to endure this and, as I mentioned, was often reduced to tears of frustration and self-loathing. It may have been physically doing me some good, but mentally it was having the opposite effect.

When my frustrations finally reached a crescendo and I 'ran away', for want of a better term, I berated myself for being weak and foolish, not sticking it out and giving up on something else yet again. But describing it now, in the kindly light of hindsight, I did the right thing. It wasn't doing me any good at all. This tool had definitely turned toxic.

So with all that in mind, why do I still believe that 'enjoyable activity' is one of the keys to a healthy state of mental health? In essence, because doing something is always better than doing nothing. All the evidence in the world might not convince me to join an aqua-salsa-spinning class but experience has shown that if I wake up with my stomach churning and a feeling of impending doom, a twenty-minute walk will give me just enough serenity to get through the day. I know from the school of hard knocks that a brisk walk will bring the overwhelming tsunami of a panic attack down to manageable proportions. I have found that on days when I do some form of activity that I enjoy (a walk in the country, a swim, some enthusiastic hoovering) I feel better than on those days I sit around feeling sorry for myself.

Yes my overanxious mind still plagues me with guilt that I 'should' be working out at 70 per cent of my maximum heart rate! Or that I 'ought' to be doing the recommended 5 x 30 minutes of aerobic exercise per week and I 'must' achieve 10 000 steps a day. I am not saying these goals are erroneous or bad for you. All I'm saying is that I want my activity to make me feel better about myself – not to wrack me with guilt.

A few months ago I applied for life assurance and was declined. The decision was based solely on my body mass index. In essence, I was too fat to insure. Feeling angry with the insurance company, I investigated further and found that there was actually only one insurance company in the whole of Great Britain that would insure someone of my weight and height. I was distraught. I knew I was fat, I knew I was morbidly obese, but this really brought home the fact that my weight could seriously affect my health.

I came home crying. My best friend walks miles and miles in a week. He walks for fitness and mental wellbeing but also to get to places, as he doesn't drive. He comforted me at the injustice of it all. Then he said, 'Let's go out for a walk. Now. Just to the end of the road and back.'

Now? Not next week? Not next month? Not after I'd read up all about exercise and drawn up a timetable to record my progress on? Now? Really?

Well I couldn't say no. It was a ten-minute walk up only a very slight incline, but I puffed and panted and nearly fainted and felt like I was going to have a heart attack. This shocked me even more than the life assurance refusal had. Not yet fifty years old and I couldn't even walk to the end of the road and back without nearly having a seizure!

'All truly great thoughts are conceived by walking.'

Friedrich Nietzsche

Since that day, we walk together regularly. I don't puff and pant quite so much and we've managed to stray further than the end of the road. We usually only have a thirty-minute stroll; we try and keep up a good pace but we're not trying to beat any records. I feel better for it and there are other benefits, too. It's quality time away from the distractions of TV and iPad; I am more aware of the changing of the seasons; it unwinds my mind and shoulders after a day spent staring at a computer screen. I would like to do more, of course I would, and I would probably feel better if I walked further or more regularly, but I do it when I can, I don't push myself to tears and my motivation for moving is as much about my mental wellbeing as it is about my physical imperfections. I'm never going to run a marathon, but I will hopefully remain active for as long as possible and will daily feel better for getting out and moving rather than sitting on the sofa 24/7.

Over to You: Move

- Get moving on a regular basis – doing something is better than doing nothing.
- Do something you enjoy – dance, walk, swim. As with diets, if the exercise regime is making you miserable it's not helping your mental health.
- Pretty much everyone can do something – I've seen ninety-year-olds doing chair-based exercises. Doing what you can is better than doing nothing at all.

Important: I am duty bound to advise you to see your GP before starting any exercise programme, especially if you have any underlying medical conditions.

Sleep

'There is a time for many words and there is a time for sleep.'

Homer

In America I didn't get enough sleep. I remember the very first day of the tour we were on the go from 7 a.m. until 1 a.m. the next morning, then we were up again six hours later. I was exhausted before the tour had even begun and I remember having a splitting headache the second day as we walked the streets of Washington. Everyone needs sleep and I seem to need much more than most people. A fact it has taken me a long time to accept.

Even now my sleep isn't restful. Last night, between the hours of dusk and dawn, I developed a brain tumour, died and came back to life miraculously recovered. Hot on the heels of that harrowing experience, I then witnessed my elderly father being attacked by some rogue traders who tried to trick money out of him on his doorstep. My dad was sobbing his heart out (something I've never seen him do in all my waking years). I called the police – no mean feat as the phone kept directing me to a pizza-delivery company – and then I helped one of the police officers escape from his bullying colleagues during a siege by smuggling information to another Force for him.

I woke up drained and discombobulated. The experiences might have been entirely of my subconscious making (and maybe I read too many books), but while I was battling with death and brain tumours and muggers and emotional parents I had no concept that it was anything other than frighteningly real. I went through a gamut of emotions from horror to fear to relief to sadness every bit as powerful as if the situations had happened in the waking world.

How terrible, you may think. And, yes, it was a relief to wake up this morning, and it has given me a renewed sense of the joy of being alive, but this is not a one-off. The night before last I had to re-sit my A levels, at the weekend a passenger plane crash landed before my very eyes, last week the world came to an end in a nuclear apocalypse, and I am frequently chased by Nazis. Or zombies. Or Nazi zombies if it's a particularly bad night!

As far as I can remember this has happened most of my adult life. Certainly as long as I have been treated for anxiety. I often wake up screaming. I now warn house guests about my nocturnal habits, after one unfortunate friend thought we were being burgled – my screams are that loud they can wake people in the next room. I hate to imagine what the neighbours think!

Given all that I have been through during my night-time years, how come I still claim that sleep is the best medicine for an anxious or depressed mind? Well, my American journey is a good enough example as any of what happens when I don't get enough sleep! I'm a ten-hours-a-night girl, ideally. I can usually survive on eight hours for a few nights a week but need a good catch-up at the weekend. If, even for one night, I get less than seven hours, I'm a crying, whimpering wreck the next day. After three weeks of burning the candle at both ends in the USA it's no wonder that I was ready to erupt.

'Sleep, even troubled, dream-filled sleep, restores our bodies and gives us energy for life's trials and tribulations. I don't know what the dreams are all about but I know that sleep helps us sort out our issues and subconsciously deal with things. It takes an enormous amount of energy being anxious all the time; even if our minds don't get a break while we're sleeping, at least our bodies do. It is so much harder to cope with things when tired.

> 'It is a common experience that a problem difficult at night is resolved in the morning after the committee of sleep has worked on it.'
>
> John Steinbeck

I am lucky in that I could sleep on a clothes line. I can sleep anytime, anywhere, day or night. It's a blessing – and a curse.

A blessing because sleep is the elixir of the gods, a curse because I often waste hours of the day just conked out on my bed. I know I need to sleep to maintain positive mental health, but sleep is also a vital part of the recovery after a panic attack or hysterical episode. Somewhere amid the Nazi-eating zombie apocalypse scenarios of dream state, my subconscious is working through whatever is worrying me during the day.

Not everyone is as lucky as me to find sleep so easy, and mental health issues are frequently associated with disrupted sleep patterns. Oversleeping during the day, lying awake at night worrying, nightmares, insomnia – sleep disorders can be a symptom that can then exacerbate the problem.

Over to You: Sleep

There are many self-help remedies to establish a good sleeping pattern, some of which are listed below. If none of these work, then it is worth seeing a GP. Don't ever underestimate the effect sleep can have on your mood and your ability to think rationally.

If you can't sleep try:

- Avoiding stimulating drinks containing caffeine or alcohol and products containing nicotine before bedtime.
- Avoiding watching TV or using a computer/tablet in the bedroom.
- Training your body clock to get up and go to bed at the same time each day.
- Mindfulness (see page 190) and/or meditation at bedtime.
- Gentle exercise and fresh air during the day.
- Making your bedroom a comfortable, quiet place that is a peaceful sanctuary away from your worries.

* * *

Three days further into the trip and I wasn't the only one on the bus who was getting ratty and upset. It's tough doing that sort of tour. If nothing else you find out a lot about yourself – your limits and your strengths. Again, with hindsight I can see that my struggles were no worse than anyone else's in that group – but I wasn't living anyone else's struggles – I was living mine.

On the day in question there was snappiness about the last of the milk being used, girls refusing to eat the meal another group had cooked, bitchiness behind the backs of people with attitude, bitchiness behind the backs of those whose faces didn't fit. By the time we'd reached Panama City (the one in Florida, not the one in Panama) the tension was palpable and all the bonhomie and forced friendliness of the first fortnight had evaporated.

I was becoming hyper-sensitive to every little thing and I can't believe I didn't see this would happen. In an amazing display of bad timing I chose this day to explain to the group my problems with anxiety, that I have problems being in a group of people and need lots of time alone. I explained that I cry a lot and I was honest about the doubts I was having about coping with the trek for another seven weeks.

Eleven out the twelve of my companions responded to my 'confession' with kindness and sensitivity. I felt supported and relieved that I had been honest about myself. That was until the twelfth person spoke up.

This young girl, still in her teens, decided to tell me that she didn't appreciate what I said and that she had come on holiday to enjoy herself and not to deal with other people's problems. She told me I needed a kick up the backside to cheer myself up and that I was being selfish. She also said that, because she had given me the benefit of her opinion, I now owed it to her to cheer up.

Over ten years later, with the benefit of experience, acceptance of myself, and time to analyse my past wearing the clear glasses of hindsight, I can see her point of view.

At the time I just crumbled.

Never mind that the rest of the group were sympathetic, it was her voice that I heard over and over in my head. Her voice that resonated with the 'nasty gnomes' that were already tearing my self-esteem and mental stability to shreds.

How I didn't pick up my backpack that night and walk away from the whole trip I will never know. I stomped about the campsite, packing my bags, sobbing and panicking. I say that I didn't listen to the kind voices of the friends around me but I must have done because they convinced me to at least stay until our next stop in New Orleans. New Orleans was a longer stay and we were booking into a guest house, so there would be potentially time to recharge our batteries and look at things more rationally. And then there was the Golden Gate Bridge. Would it be any easier to get there on my own? Would I ever realise my dream?

I woke the next morning gutted, depressed and shattered emotionally and physically – but I got on the bus. Sadly, the atmosphere had become so bad that another team member did leave the tour that very morning. I never found out what happened to him. I often wonder how my adventure would have turned out if I had jumped ship (van) then and there.

We arrived in the French Quarter of New Orleans on a sweaty, humid evening. I was miserable and homesick. I forgot to mention that another teenage member of the trip was constantly, day and night, calling me a 'Bible Bashing Jesus Freak' even though I've never bashed a Bible in my life! He thought it was funny. I was not amused. Inside I felt hollow, lonely, afraid and desperate to go home.

I just wanted to get away from anyone and everyone. I was afraid of them. I told the group organiser that I was booking into a hotel room on my own. The room was fairly basic as hotel rooms go, but to me it was heavenly luxury. It had crisp clean white sheets, cable TV, a hot shower all of my own and air-conditioning. I got myself clean, I slept, I watched reruns of *Friends*, I washed my clothes in the hotel laundry and I emailed home.

Not just home but everyone I knew. I told them about the trek and hostility and the amazing things we had seen, the amazing things we would still see if I stuck it out; I didn't want to give up, I had worked hard to get there. I needed to prove to myself that I could do it. I wanted to see Texas and the Grand Canyon, the Alamo and Monument Valley. I had paid for another 10 000 miles of experiences, but I felt panicky and shaky at the thought of staying on that crowded bus for another minute let alone another seven weeks. Sitting in an internet booth on a hot, Deep South August night, that dream of the Golden Gate Bridge seemed even further away than ever.

I slept again, deeply and comfortably (hooray for the healing balm of sleep!) and I revelled in the solitude of my own hotel room. I had another day and another night to think things through. I wandered up and down Bourbon Street and other parts of the touristy area. I passed voodoo shops and topless bars with a vague curiosity and ate genuine jambalaya because it's delicious but also because it's what you 'do' in New Orleans (if you're not into voodoo or topless bars).

Along with the email, I also rang my poor long-suffering dad. If I was too old to be 'trekking' round America, he was definitely too old to be getting hysterical phone calls from his thirty-something daughter…

'Dad – I'm in New Orleans and I need you to come and get me,' I sobbed down the phone.

'I can't come and get you. You're five thousand miles away,' he said calmly, although I know he is every bit the worrier I am and must have been fraught at the other end of the phone.

'But I can't cope – it was a mistake, I need to come home,' I wailed repeatedly.

'You can't come home – you need to be brave – you can do it.'

Well that's a shortened version of the long pep talk he gave me from the other side of the Atlantic. Honestly, who knows what to say to a loved one who is in such a state of panic and so far away? Many years later my brother was taken into hospital in Melbourne, Australia, and I felt some of the helplessness and fear that my dad must have felt that day.

When I returned, later that day, to check my emails I was astounded at the support and encouragement I received from my friends and family. My brother told me that the 'disasters' on a journey are the experiences that make the best stories when we get home. They also make us better people. My mum reminded me of the Golden Gate Bridge and told me she believed I could do it.

'"Disasters" on our journey are the experiences that make the best stories when we get home. They also make us better people.'

Dave Lockwood

I wanted to cry (yet again) and I wanted to be at home, but somehow (and I really can't remember how) I decided to stick it out. If people at home loved me what could a couple of cold-hearted, cruel travelling companions do to hurt me?

Getting on the bus the next morning was the hardest but the best thing I'd ever done. By that time a second person had left the tour, so in many ways I was a survivor! It was a long journey to our next stop in San Antonio. Spirits were subdued. A second person abandoning the tour had shocked us all. I can't say for sure what was going on in the minds of everyone else but somewhere near the Texas border there was an unspoken change in the mood. We changed the CD from Kid Rock to Johnny Cash and Willie Nelson, more melancholy than angry, and I guess we were all alone with our thoughts. We had eleven hours in the van that day, which may or may not have been a good thing, but by the evening, in the campsite, the mood had lightened. There was a lot of teasing, game-playing and sabotaging of tents, which may be childish but it sure as hell beats bitchiness and backstabbing.

In San Antonio we went out for an 'all you can eat' Chinese buffet, which perked everyone up, and afterwards we all sat on top of the bus and talked. There were some apologies and a lot of honesty. We all agreed that we needed to leave the past behind us and make the rest of the trip the best ever. Somehow these past few days had brought us closer together. We came up with some suggestions to 'spread the love' and decided on a Secret Summer Santa, planning a party night with balloons and presents and games and cocktails. My fear and dread began to be replaced with warmth and fuzziness.

The next three weeks passed in a blur of highs and lows but with no major calamities. Santa Fe, Durango, Moab, Monument Valley and the Grand Canyon. All places I had only ever dreamed of visiting, these were my reward for sticking with it. Then on to Las Vegas where I placed a bet in a casino and rode in a white limo before we headed into California and finally… Mum's prediction was close to becoming fulfilled… after seven thousand miles on the road in a tiny minibus with only strangers for company, we arrived in San Francisco.

I never thought I would make it, so it was a real celebration day of how much I'd achieved in the past couple of years. It couldn't have been a better experience. The trek company had organised an evening cruise under the Golden Gate Bridge. I was so excited and so proud of myself that I bought champagne for everyone and we drank it as the sun set on the beautiful surroundings of San Francisco Bay. I had told the group why this was such a special moment for me and everyone shared in my celebration.

Later that evening I went out to 'swing a wooden leg' with one of the Danish girls on the tour. 'Swing a wooden leg' is a Danish term for going out for a few drinks. We actually had a great time and we met lots of interesting people including a man who flew planes for the US air force, a Scottish poker player and someone from Leicester (well, not everyone you meet can be exciting!). I had such a good night, I felt young again and was amazed that I was able to speak to so many strangers. It was another great confidence boost. I felt powerful, I had conquered my fears and I thought I could accomplish anything.

After my 'Everest Experience' in San Francisco there were still five weeks left of the tour as we headed into Canada and the northern states of the USA. There was plenty of bitchiness, backstabbing and challenges still to come, but I had changed as a person and, although they still got me down, I dealt with them more rationally and assertively. It really is a novel in itself, one which I may write some day when I have several free months to jot it all down.

In the final pages of my diary of my trip I noted how much people had changed, even the girl who had been so cutting to me in Panama City, and my diary records: 'She has changed so much since the beginning of the trip and I guess that's what travelling is all about, not who you are when you start the journey but who you are when you end it.' Thinking about it now, ten years later, I realise that that is true of so many experiences, and even of life itself – it's not who you are when you start the journey but who you are at the end that matters.

It's not who you are when you start the journey but who you are at the end that matters.

I flew home from JFK ten weeks after I had arrived a different person. I was ready to take on the world. I truly believed that my anxious days were behind me. I was about to move house to

Nottingham and start a teacher-training course and was ready
for it. For one of the very few times in my life I was full of calm
confidence and not fear. I could cope with anything life threw at
me! What could possibly go wrong?

I'd reached the Golden Gate Bridge but had I changed as a
person? Would I ever start a job and stick to it without leaving in
a blaze of ignominy? Would I be able to find peace with myself
and with other people? Had I tamed the tiger of anxiety that
plagued my life, had the black hole of depression been lifted for
ever?

Of course that isn't the end of the story. Life was about to
throw its worst at me and within a year I was very nearly back at
square one.

CHAPTER FIVE

Count Your Blessings

I thought I had 'arrived' when I sailed under the Golden Gate Bridge as the sun set on a summer evening. I thought my problems were behind me and the only way was up. I thought wrong. Almost exactly a year later I was back in the States, sobbing my heart out and bemoaning my woes.

In downtown Manhattan, next to the site of the World Trade Center, is 'The Little Chapel that Stood'. St Paul's Chapel, which has been situated on the same site since the days of George Washington, and which continued to stand as its younger and much larger neighbours were reduced to rubble on 11 September 2001. That this tiny building wasn't crushed or squashed on that disastrous day is remarkable in itself, but what happened there over the following few months is the true miracle. A testament to what is good and honourable in human nature and how that spirit, if not able to defeat the powers of evil, will at least never be destroyed by it.

For months after 9/11 this little chapel never once closed its doors. It was staffed day and night by willing volunteers who provided beds, food, counselling, practical help as well as love and support to the hundreds of emergency workers dealing with the aftermath of the Twin Towers tragedy.

When I visited three years after the disaster, much of this work was still in evidence. Thousands of letters of support lined the walls, moving tributes to the workers and victims. There was also a deep sense of spirituality and other-worldliness pervading the building, which even the hardened atheist would have struggled to deny.

It was here I sat crying for nigh on two hours. I would like to say I was mourning the troubles of the world – and there was an element of that – but in truth my own self-pity had once again got the better of me. I was feeling sorry for myself!

* * *

I had been euphoric when I arrived home from my marathon ten-week trek nearly a year before. I had achieved the impossible. I had overcome many obstacles – beaten my fears. Life from that point on was going to be a breeze. I came back to Britain full of confidence and expectation. Everything was back on track. My mental illness was behind me. Nothing could possibly go wrong from now on – I was invincible!

Wrong!

As children we are fed fairy tales that make us believe in happy endings. As adults we are fed makeover programmes, magazine articles and adverts which make us believe that, with just a couple of small changes, our lives can be perfect. Of course it doesn't work like that. Nothing is ever simple and nothing worth having comes about instantly. I know that now… I didn't know it then, when I stepped off the aeroplane from my Great American Adventure ready to move home to Nottingham and begin my Great Teaching Adventure.

Yes, becoming a secondary science teacher might not have been the best option for someone with a diagnosis of social phobia, but then neither was a trek around America and I truly believed it was my destiny. I was determined at that point in my life that I wasn't going to be the 'weak mental crazy woman'. Yes, I'd had a few bad years and a multitude of fears but I truly believed I was 'cured' and that that episode of my life was behind me. Maybe I chose teaching, secondary school teaching no less, because it was one of the most stressful jobs I could think of? Surely if I could do that I had proved I could do anything. I could have featured in one of those magazine makeovers: FROM SOCIAL PHOBIA TO SCIENCE TEACHER the headline would have read. They could have had pictures of me under the Golden Gate Bridge, drinking champagne, with an inset of me hiding behind a locked door as my 'before' photo. It would have made a good spread.

Things went well for a while. I moved into a new house back in Nottingham, where I had lived for most of my life, and quickly made new friends and became reacquainted with old ones. I started my teacher-training course at Derby University and got on really well. Public speaking has never been one of my phobias and even today I would rather give a lecture to a thousand people than have a difference of opinion with one colleague at work. Mental illness knows no logic. I had (still have) a natural propensity for teaching and on a good day I felt no fear at standing in front of a class of recalcitrant teenagers and, fresh from my confidence-building US trip, there were many good days. I received excellent reviews from my teaching practices, fantastic feedback from my peers, a terrific buzz from standing in front of a class. In short, I was happy, confident and once again I was going places.

Then, one evening, while I was preparing a lesson about photosynthesis for a year-nine class, I received a phone call.

For many years I had feared the telephone ringing, feared answering it. Refused to answer it on many days, unplugged it on many more. That evening I had no such reservations. I was flying high. This was my time to shine – surely nothing could drag me back to the depths I had previously visited?

My mum had been ill for a few months prior to that phone call. They had diagnosed her with cancer of the oesophagus. I had been with her when she got the diagnosis but I really wasn't worried. She had already beaten breast cancer and skin cancer, and besides, it was other people's mums who had serious illnesses, not mine. When I had seen her that Christmas, four months after my American Adventure and six weeks before The Phone Call, she was on top form. Yes she had lost weight and was wearing a wig from the chemotherapy, but she was the life and soul of the party. Her energy put me to shame. In fact on Christmas afternoon she left me at home and went out to a party with the comment, 'You won't enjoy it – I'll go on my own.' She was probably right. I stayed in and had a post-Christmas dinner siesta. To me she was receiving treatment, she was on the mend, she was only sixty-three.

Then that February the phone rang and it was left to my brother to tell me the worst possible news. That she literally had only weeks, if not days, left to live.

She was in Essex and I was in Nottingham, so I quickly agreed time off my studies and teaching placement to be with her at the end. My brother and I stayed with her most days and some nights for nearly three weeks. We watched old episodes of *Dad's Army* with her, which she chuckled at in between dozing off. We played her favourite Daniel O'Donnell CDs until we were fed up with the sound of them and we dripped Olbas Oil onto her pillow to help her breathe. She was comfortable for most of the time and, bizarrely, those few weeks were some of the closest I ever had with her.

It could have been a perfect end (if any ending is perfect at such a young age); we got time to say goodbye, she wasn't in pain and I really don't think she knew what was going on. She had plenty of visitors, she was popular and well-loved. It was a bittersweet time with plenty of laughter, a few tears and one incident which would haunt me for years to come.

* * *

My brother was always mum's favourite. I don't say that with any resentment. He was *everyone's* favourite. He was *my* favourite. As a boy he was cute, with ash-blonde hair in a pudding bowl cut; he was entertaining, friendly, outgoing. All the things I wasn't. I was sullen, introvert, afraid. He was intelligent too. He seemed to be able to converse about almost any subject whereas I would stutter and mumble through even topics I knew inside out. But he wasn't big-headed. He was humble, sensitive and kind. He would, still will, put himself out for anyone. Everyone loves Dave, and he deserves it. It wasn't a bone of contention to me that I was second best, it was just a fact of life.

At my mum's end, he was there doing the things I couldn't do. Oh, I was there, too. I talked to her and kept her company and fetched the nurse if something needed 'doing'. But Dave was really 'there' with her. He stroked her head, cooed at her, nursed her, loved her. I wasn't jealous. I was glad she had someone to do the things I didn't have it in me to do.

She was doped up on morphine, which might explain what happened, but I don't believe that. To me it was a confirmation of something I had known all my life.

On one long day in that room where Mum spent her final hours, we were chatting together, Dave on one side of the bed, me on the other. Daniel O'Donnell was crooning from the CD player in the corner. The mood was contented and peaceful.

'I love you Dave,' Mum whispered to my brother.

'I love you too,' he replied.

That's where I should have left it. I knew the status quo. There was no need to poke the wound with a big stick. Why didn't I just leave it there? If I live to be a hundred I will never know why I didn't just leave it there!

'Do you love me too?' The words were out of my mouth before I could even regret thinking them. I knew the answer. I didn't need to open this particular Pandora's Box.

'No,' she said and turned back to my brother as I sat in stunned silence feeling the hospital room recede into unreality as I digested what she had just said.

So it was out there. In black and white. The truth. Of course there is no rule that says a mother has to love her daughter and I wasn't very easy to love. Did I love her? I don't honestly know. Not in the way I love other members of my family, so maybe I got the answer I deserved.

I continued to sit by my mum until the end, continued to make peace with her in my own way. I remembered the 'love' she had put into the Golden Gate gift and I had to admit it was Mum who had got me off my backside and heading Stateside. I tried my best to show love and later on she did try to take back what she had said. Maybe it *was* the morphine talking, but the trouble was that one word 'No' backed up every experience I could remember of my relationship with my mum. I wasn't what she had 'ordered'. I didn't come out right. I wasn't outgoing enough, friendly enough, cuddly enough, normal enough! In short, I just wasn't lovable enough.

* * *

So five months later I sat crying in The Little Chapel That Stood while the World Trade Center crumbled. I was angry... at life? At God? At myself? Who knows?

Mum had died peacefully and nearly a hundred people came to say their goodbyes at her funeral. I was sad, I was angry, I grieved, and a small child inside me was relieved. There is so much talk of closure nowadays, and there had been a closure of sorts, at the side of that Chelmsford Hospital bed, but there had been no healing, just a gouging open of old wounds which would take years to remedy.

After the funeral I tucked all those feelings neatly away, I don't quite know how, but I was determined to finish my teaching course. My mum would have wanted me to, she would have been proud of me, just as she'd been so proud when I reached the Golden Gate Bridge, if not more so. At least I can feel content that Mum died seeing my life back on track; even if it wasn't to last, at least at that point she could rest easy thinking that the worst of my troubles were behind me.

Of course, deep-seated feelings of grief and self-loathing can't be hidden for long. I finished the course, passed with flying colours, then I took a trip with a friend, paid for by an insurance policy of my mum's (yet again my dear mum helped me fulfil my dreams). I guess I was trying to recreate the 'highs' of the previous summer. Instead, in the 'Capital of the World' with time to reflect and remember, all my old pity and negativity resurfaced.

There is an old, old story of Jacob who wrestled all night with God. He would not cease saying, 'I will not let you go until you bless me.' It was like that for me that afternoon in St Paul's Chapel. I don't know how long I would have sat there, or even if at that point I believed there was a God to hear my tears, but I wasn't going to budge until I received some sort of answer. Answers to the eternal question 'Why'?

Why had I got to the Golden Gate Bridge only to have my life crumble to pieces a year later?

Why had my mum got ill just as I was getting my life back on track?

Why hadn't my mum loved me?

Why was I such an unlovable, miserable, failure of a creature?

Why had two planes been allowed to cause so much destruction in Manhattan?

Why was life such a struggle?

I cried, I sat, I wrestled, I cried some more. For two hours I bemoaned my woes. Mostly, I felt sorry for myself. Even though my troubles were minimal compared to many others who were using that chapel as refuge, my biggest, selfish wail was 'Why me?'

Did God answer me that day? I wouldn't be so bold as to claim that, but something monumental happened. Suddenly in the middle of all my sorrowful questioning, from out of the Slough of Despond where I was just about as forlorn and hopeless as I could sink, a new thought popped into my head, so clear it was as if a voice had spoken to me from beyond myself…

'Count your blessings.'

What? This didn't fit with all my self-pity. There was nothing to be grateful for! Absolutely nothing! Hasn't anyone been listening? I'm hard done by! The universe is out to get me! I'm a worm! Lower than a worm! Worms have a purpose – I am a piteous, pathetic, wretched… maggot!

Then it came again, unbidden, into my mind…

'Count your blessings.'

Was this my subconscious speaking to me or some omnipotent power? We can debate that until the cows come home, but whatever it was it somehow, against all reason, took me out of the spiral of despair. I started, reluctantly at first, to count my blessings.

'Well, I do have a dad and brother who love me… and lots of friends who seem to think I'm OK,' I started off tentatively. 'And, yes it was a struggle with my mum's death but I still passed my teacher-training course… and I got a job at the end of it. And hey! I'm in New York, best city in the world!' I sniffled.

Once I got started I realised that I had plenty to be thankful for, I just needed to see it. I was in good health physically, and even my mental health had come a long way in the past five years. I'd had some amazing travel experiences, I had come into enough money from my mum not to have to scrape by anymore. And, you know, maybe she did love me in her own way. She stuck by me when I was at my lowest, when many people didn't, and she gave me the dream that set me on the path to recovery.

Tips from my Toolbox: My Positive Book

When I hear songs like Paolo Nutini's 'Pencil Full of Lead' or Bobby McFerrin's 'Don't Worry be Happy' I get envious of people who are life's natural optimists, who can always see the bright side and expect events to turn out for the best. Somehow, whatever happens, these people are never disappointed. (They are also the sorts of people who probably have no understanding of mental health issues, but that's for another chapter.)

Even at my best I'm a 'glass half-empty' sort of girl. In fact my glass isn't so much 'half-empty' as 'glass dropped on the floor and smashed into little pieces!' I don't want to be, I try so hard not to be, but my natural disposition is to look for calamity and catastrophe at every turn. At my worst, when my anxiety or depression have yet again got the better of me, I become the world's worst prophet of disaster and devastation. I'm sure I'm not alone; after all, anxiety is driven by fear that the worst possible outcome is the most likely and depression is the sure and certain knowledge that we are living in the worst of times. On days like these the awful scenarios and sickening future events are played out in my mind over and over again. Either that or I will look back at situations through a grey twisted filter and build the slightest, most innocuous comment or facial expression into a declaration of war that will consume and defeat me.

It has never come naturally to me to 'count my blessings' the way I did in the New York chapel that summer. I am very good at counting my woes, but counting my blessings takes disciplined effort.

A few years back, when I was in one of my most negative of phases, a friend suggested that things weren't as gloomy as I was painting them. Of course I didn't believe her; she couldn't see things from where I was standing! She suggested that, every time something positive, enjoyable or enriching happened, I put a little sticker in my diary (she was a primary-school teacher – they like little stickers!).

I was cynical, but I was also desperate. I believed that around every corner I turned there was a snare waiting to entrap me. I was certain that every person I met had evil intentions to harm and destroy me. I couldn't see any good in any situation, so I didn't see the need for many stickers. With little hope of success I tried my friend's idea. More to prove her wrong and be able to shut her up with a triumphant 'I told you so' than any belief it would actually work. Then someone smiled at me in a shop, so I stuck a sticker in my diary; I got a phone call from a friend, another sticker; I took a walk in the sunshine, sticker; I laughed at my favourite TV programme, sticker. After a week my diary was full of colourful stickers. I remembered the time as depressing, hostile and useless, but my sticker diary told me otherwise.

I learned from that week that I have to force myself to look for the good. My dysfunctional subconscious isn't going to do it for me.

Now I have taken the sticker diary one step further. Beside my bed I keep a positive notebook and every evening I write in it the positive things which have happened that day. Some days it's easy: if the sun is shining, if I've done something enjoyable or productive, or just if I'm in a positive mood. Other days it is much harder, not that there aren't a million things for me to be positive about in every day, just that sometimes they get obscured by the grey twisted filter.

I always force myself to do it, though. Every single night – even if to me it seems like the day from hell. I do it even if I've hidden in bed with fear, even if I've run out of work screaming. It's a discipline that to other people comes as natural as breathing but in which I have to train myself. I find it important to write the things down. Somehow it makes them more real, but also, when I'm down and feel that my life is a useless waste of space, I can look back on my positive book and it gives me clear evidence that there are many things to smile about.

> 'Every day might not be good but there is something good in every day.'
>
> Alice Morse Earle

Through some of the hours and hours of counselling I have had over the years I have learned some important lessons. One is not to label events, days or relationships but to accept the good and bad that they inevitably bring. To say 'I'm having a really stressful day' can often become a self-fulfilling prophesy. By labelling the day as stressful I automatically become more anxious, my negative filter kicks up a gear and I look out for more stressful disasters to confirm my prediction. Negative labelling is a difficult habit to break but I have found that, if I can teach myself to do it, life is much easier, and I can look at things with calmer eyes. To help stop myself labelling I use a mental version of my positive book. If I have some event which I am dreading or if even getting out of bed is proving too difficult I will sometimes make myself do this positive note-taking mentally, so that even in the bad situations I can see there is always something good to notice or smile about.

In Corrie Ten Boom's autobiography *The Hiding Place*, Corrie talks about her time in Ravensbrück, a World War Two concentration camp. In this true story Corrie is placed in a ghastly dormitory, cramped with thousands of other unwashed and diseased prisoners, lying on a straw mattress with eight other women and doing hard physical labour every day. Worst of all, the place is infested with fleas.

Corrie's sister Betsie urges Corrie to be grateful for everything they are experiencing, even the fleas. Corrie has a great faith but even she finds being thankful for fleas a step too far.

A few days later Corrie comes back from working in the fields to Betsie who was on light duties dues to ill health. Betsie was really excited and couldn't wait to explain the reason to Corrie. You see, in the room that was shared sleeping quarters for a large number of women they were surprised at how much freedom they were given and couldn't understand why the guards always left them alone when they were in the dormitory and never came to investigate what the group of women were doing. It turned out that none of the guards would set foot in the room for one very simple reason:

'Because of the fleas!' That's what she said. 'That place is crawling with fleas!'

My mind rushed back to our first hour in this place. I remembered Betsie's bowed head, remembered her thanks to God for creatures I could see no use for.

From *The Hiding Place* by Corrie Ten Boom

Now I think if Corrie and Betsie could be grateful for fleas in a place like Ravensbrück, I'm sure there are many things I can feel grateful and positive about in my safe and comfortable twenty-first-century home.

Over to You: Your Positive Book

- What do you have in your life that's positive? A home; a pet; laughter? Make a mental list of all that is good about you and your life.
- Try keeping a positive notebook and use stickers or write every day at least one positive thing that has happened.

- Do this every day. If being positive doesn't come naturally to you, all the more reason to train yourself to look for the good in every situation.
- It will be difficult to spot the good things at first but you will see them if you persevere. Don't be swayed by the grey twisted filter; simply count your blessings.
- Avoid broad-brush statements like 'today is really stressful,' 'everything is going wrong.' 'I've ruined everything.' Train yourself instead to see what went well.
- Keep your diary as evidence that even a time in your life that you thought was bleak had its positive moments.

* * *

If there is one thing that I have learned about life it is that it is unpredictable. None of us know what is around the next bend. If there is one thing I learned about myself at that particular crossroads in my life, it was that I was ill-equipped mentally and emotionally to deal with life's twists and turns. It took me two years of counselling and hours of soul searching to reach any kind of peace about my mum's passing. During those two years my chronic anxiety and phobias were to resurface with a vengeance. I often felt I had been ignominiously deposited back at square one, but in truth I was growing as a person, learning to accept my weaknesses and getting acquainted with the real me.

You'll never get where you are going if you only travel on sunny days.

Fridge magnet

Through the grief, shock and anguish of my mum's sudden death, which was surely one of the low points of my life, came the seeds of many lessons I needed to absorb. There came a new appreciation to value what we have every minute, because we never know when it might be gone, and there came a growing acceptance that things are never as perfect as we want them to be but that they can be pretty wonderful just the way they are.

For the first time in my life I was beginning to understand and value the Life Less Lived.

CHAPTER SIX

The Long Road to Healing Is Worth a Thousand Miracle Cures

What do people want out of life? What are their aims? Their ambitions? Their hopes and dreams? For most of us, myself included (I don't pretend to be some kind of spiritual hyper-being), we would say money and/or health and/or happiness and/or good looks and/or good friends or maybe a combination of all these. Our priorities change throughout our lives. I wanted to be pretty when I was eighteen much more than I'm bothered about it now, but I think anybody who is honest would say that these are the goals most people aspire to.

The problem is that life, in all its infinite forms, is a lottery. Some of us will never be good looking or rich. One day we may be healthy, the next we may be lying on an operating table fighting for our lives. We may have been born into the family from hell, and some days (or even most days) we can feel miserable for no apparent reason. So we aim for things which are out of our control and then we feel we have failed when we are overdrawn, depressed, get ill or when friends let us down. Then we get anxious. Then we get more depressed. Then we watch a couple of TV ads with slim, happy people buying things we can't afford and we think, 'Why me?' because it seems as though we are the only ones who feel like this.

When we give up or run away or spend a day under the duvet hiding from the world we feel we are wasting our lives, well I do anyway. True, these days won't bring us more money or more friends or help us lose that extra couple of stone that will surely make us slim and happy. If life is all about getting money, being healthy and happy, feeling good about our appearance and having good relationships with our nearest and dearest then 99 per cent of the population are complete failures!

And this is the crux of *Loving the Life Less Lived*. Because most people on the Life Less Lived road (no, strike that – just most people, full stop) don't have enough money, they fall out with their friends and have long-standing resentments about their family. Most of us on this journey know what it is to experience real ill health, loss and unhappiness and, let's face it, Life Less Lived folk are never going to be called the Beautiful People, not in the rest of the world's eyes anyway.

And yet we are beautiful. Some of the most wonderful, kind, attractive, stunning and downright gorgeous people I have ever met would never make it into a perfume advert, they don't have a big house or a flashy car, or fifty-seven grandchildren who dote on their every word. They are ordinary people like you and me, who have been thrown every unlucky break that life can dream up, who've been down in the pits of despair and are still holding on. These are the beautiful people. These are the people who know what is really important in life.

Never did I experience this more than in the two summers I spent in Brazil. One summer was full of amazing 'highs' that yet again fooled me into thinking I was invincible, the next summer, through no fault but my own mental failings, I crashed and burned.

The summer after my mum died I had wanted to go to Brazil with a short-term mission organisation. I applied and was rejected. They believed it was too soon after my mum's death. I thought they were wrong, so I went to New York instead. They were right of course; I probably realised that somewhere around the time I was sobbing in St Paul's Chapel. I applied to the same organisation again the next summer, after I had spent a year teaching, and was this time accepted.

The preceding year, my first as a qualified teacher, was not without event. I taught chemistry to A level students and I survived until the end of the year. Looking back I take that as a huge achievement. It wasn't a school full of accommodating, eager to learn teenagers, but then again nobody got attacked with a Bunsen burner or hydrochloric acid, either! Not while I was there anyway. I learned much about the stronger parts of my personality that year. I walked into the classroom every day with confidence and authority. I spent about as many hours crying in the staff room. I had lots of ailments, flu, tonsillitis, migraines, and I was constantly exhausted. Anyone who ever says to me that teachers have it easy will get very short shrift. Five or six hours performing in front of rebellious youths trying to get them interested in covalent bonding followed by three or four hours every evening planning lessons, preparing resources and searching around for the mental resilience to do it again the next day... but I finished the year!

True, it was getting harder and harder to convince myself that my 'mental' days were behind me and I think my colleagues heaved a sigh of relief when I left at the end of the summer term. Again I made the excuse that it was because I wanted to teach younger children; it wasn't that I couldn't cope, not at all! Who me? Of course I could cope! I'm an invincible superwoman whose time spent hiding behind her front door was a mere blip in my life plan. Not the real me at all!

So I spent the next two summers in the favelas of São Paulo. It is something I have always wanted to do and I am so pleased that I was able to achieve it, even if it didn't turn out at all how I'd planned it. I went with the idea that a group of (relatively) rich and talented people from a First World country would visit a developing nation to give them the gift of our wisdom and expertise. We visited the shanty towns that the guide books suggest you avoid. Quite often they are policed by the drug gangs rather than the actual police. In our induction we were told that if we were kidnapped no ransom would be paid. We were literally taking our life in our hands. And yet time after time over those two summers it was proved to me that I was the needy person and the Brazilians, in their ramshackled slums and tenements, were the ones with the true riches. I was to receive much more than I could ever give back to my Brazilian friends.

'Some people are so poor, all they have is money.'

Anon

Brazil is a country of contrasts where multimillionaires live next door to some of the poorest people on the planet. You can come out of a mall full of Gucci and Calvin Klein and a hundred yards down the street find corrugated iron houses held together with duct tape all balanced on top of one another. Many buildings in the city centre of São Paulo have helipads on their roofs, allegedly because the super-rich business executives don't want to see the poverty in the favelas as they drive to work. They simply pretend it isn't there.

I had a real epiphany one day during my first summer in São Paulo. We had been working in a favela in the south of the city. São Paulo is a large city housing over twenty million people. On this particular day we had a trip to visit another favela further north. We had thought where we were staying was poor but nothing prepared me for what I was about to see. I walked through the lowest level of poverty I have ever experienced. Homes stapled together from faded billboards and rotting MDF, crammed full of families and scrapyard leftovers. Rough dirt the only carpet, a tattered and ragged sheet for the door. Children playing barefoot with broom handles and plastic bags for toys, creased and worn women huddled together in alleyways. The toxic smell of sewage drenching the air.

The cruellest irony to strike me was that this complex of battered homes existed (still exists) under a motorway overpass. For twenty miles in every direction sprawls the mammoth conurbation of São Paulo. These beautiful children have never seen a green field or watched a butterfly land on a flower or smelled new mown grass. For all the days of their lives the only splendour of creation that will exist for them lies in this favela, with the world driving by overhead, oblivious.

In that moment I hurt for the whole of humanity. Not even so much for the people who live like this but for what it takes for the rest of us to drive by and not care. Even now I am still driving by; yes, I went back the next summer, but let's face it I am much more concerned about what ridiculous presents to buy people for Christmas this year or that my broadband bill is too high than I ever am for those people. On that day, if only for a moment, I wanted to save the world – but how easy it is to forget and want only to save myself.

That day, out of everything I saw I remember one thing. I walked down one particular alley, box homes on either side, which opened onto a wider track. There before me, daubed in faded red paint, 'Deus é fiel', God is faithful. The irony of it made me sick and angry. How could anyone who lives there have any sort of faith in God let alone believe that he is faithful back?

That was just one incident in a plethora of similar experiences I had in Brazil. If I am on The Road Less Travelled, my Brazilian friends are the tour guides. They have been along the road, got the T-shirt. They know all about the joys that can be found when you are struggling to survive. It is a paradox that I still do not fully understand, I wish everyone in the world had a happy home with a roof that doesn't leak, running water and a separate room to cook in and another to sleep in. And yet those that don't have any of these things seem to have so much. How can that be?

I have a thousand tales from São Paulo of kindness, generosity, of people giving thanks in the face of appalling adversity, but I will tell you just one more. It was a Saturday and we were visiting a small church a three-mile walk from our lodgings. I had a bad cold and the heat and the noise of the children's group we were leading (imagine thirty excited kids all shouting in Portuguese) had given me a migraine. I felt sick. The hall we were working in was no bigger than my living room at home. We had craft activities and colouring pencils, which were like wonders from heaven to these children whose only toy most of the time was their imagination. Time after time in Brazil (and in the rest of my life) my weakness exposed me. I was not some great teacher and missionary from the Western world. I was a weak girl who cried for her family and bemoaned her woes at any chance she got.

The pastor lived in an even smaller room behind the church. There was an outdoor toilet, small and cold, with a shower head above it. I don't know how they managed to wash themselves – there was hardly room to get in and close the door behind – but this was the family's bathroom. In the living area there was a small cooking and eating area then a curtain behind which was a double bed that the whole family slept in. It was tiny. It was nothing. These people had nothing to offer – I repeat NOTHING to offer and yet there was the pastor's wife cooking a red bean stew and rice for the four English girls who had turned up on their doorstep with feeble ambitions to 'help'.

It was obvious I was poorly and so the pastor and his wife offered a lie down in their 'bedroom' while the children's group was going on. I protested. I was embarrassed. It seemed to me that we had already imposed on their time and space enough without me snoring in the only place they had to call their own. I was ready to be very English about the whole thing and refuse the offer but our translator told me it would be very rude to refuse and they would be offended, so I gratefully lay down on the bed, looking up at holes in the ceiling crammed with plastic bags to stop the rain coming in. A thin curtain separated me from the pastor's wife happily cooking for her guests. At that moment I felt – I don't know – somehow I felt, no I knew, that they were the ones with so much to give and we had, in every way that mattered, nothing to give at all.

If Brazil taught me anything it was that true beauty is kindness and love and not perfect skin and a size-ten body; that life is about collecting experiences and wisdom not material riches; that the only career path that truly matters is the one we take inside ourselves to discover humanity's grace and strength; and that struggles and challenges along the way can, if we let them, be windows to all that is good and joyful in the world. They are tools to help us grow into the people we were always meant to be. To hone our creativity, to give us strength, to show our weaknesses and help us love ourselves as well as loving others who are failing and falling and are just not as perfect as we need them to be.

Imagine if we had ambitions to be wise, courageous and joyful instead of rich, successful and happy? Would the way we approach life's ups and downs change?

'You don't develop courage by being happy in your relationships every day. You develop it by surviving difficult times and challenging adversity.'

Epicurus

For years I hoped and prayed for overnight healing, angels from heaven, wondrous experiences I could shout from the rooftops. None of that ever happened. My miracle was that, although I have found living inside my head a constant struggle, every day I have had just as much strength as I needed to get me through to the next day. Moreover, my miracle was that on the days (and weeks and years) when I felt I was wasting my life, that I couldn't go on, on those days I learned lessons. I grew. I didn't know it was happening of course; you can't see your fingernails growing and you can't see your soul gaining strength, but drop by minuscule drop I developed character, learned to love, healed my old wounds. I am so thankful I never woke up one morning and was better. I am more thankful than you will ever know for those down-and-out days when nothing went right. These are the days which made me who I am today. All the momentous, noteworthy learning experiences in my life have come when I was at rock bottom, in crisis and despair. Looking back it is these experiences that I am most thankful for in my life – not the times when things were easy or straightforward. If I learned from my weaknesses that first summer in Brazil, I was to have much more learning, weakness and wasted time on my second visit.

Tips from my Toolbox: Self-Help Books (or just books!)

Today a friend posted a photo on Facebook (you've gotta love Facebook for sharing wisdom, news and pictures of people's Sunday dinners!). It said:

Five steps to being a happier person:

1. Read more books
2. Read more books
3. Read more books
4. Read more books
5. Read more books.

From *Weird Things Customers Say in Bookshops*, by Jen Campbell

I find this so true, books can transport us to other worlds; they can inform, educate and humble us. They can inspire us and transform us. They can form a porthole out of our miserable humdrum existence or hold a mirror up to reflect the beauty that is in our lives.

But what of the genre of 'self-help' books? For a long time these have had a bad press. I'm not sure why. Maybe they are perceived as preying on people's vulnerabilities or maybe those who deride them do so because they see themselves as 'strong' – and not needing help at all let alone 'self-help'. They are probably the same people who say that us lesser mortals with mental health issues should just 'snap out of it' and 'pull ourselves together'. Whoever 'they' are and whatever 'they' say, if you find a method (or a book) that helps you, then use it. It isn't a weakness to take support when it is on offer, and if that support costs little and doesn't impinge on anyone else's time or resources then all the better.

Having said that, there are many caveats I would add to the use of self-help books. First, if you think you are experiencing depression, an anxiety disorder or any other mental health condition then books are no substitute for a trip to the GP. Strangely though, many GPs will now offer books/websites/self-help as the first line of treatment. Recently, before I was offered any talking therapies, I was given the web addresses of several organisations where I could seek help myself. In the same way, a friend was once referred to a mental health practitioner in the hope of receiving some grief counselling, he was told instead to go to the library and borrow a book! Both these experiences left us feeling frustrated and alone. When you are at rock bottom you need someone to help, you don't have the energy, motivation or strength of will to DIY it. I'm sure many people don't even have it in them to go back to the GP and ask for something more. They fall through the gaps.

As I mentioned right at the beginning of the book, when I set out on this journey there were precious few self-help books to choose from. Now the choice is overwhelming. The fact that it is such a growth market is proof to me of how many people experience anxiety and depression. In my early twenties, when I was first diagnosed with depression, the internet meant nothing to anyone except computer science geeks; now there are websites, forums and podcasts by the bucket-load to give advice, solace and practical tips.

Having spent more money than I care to remember on self-help books in the intervening years, my view of them can be summed up by paraphrasing Barry Norman when he said, 'I love children but I couldn't eat a whole one.' So it is for me:

'I love self-help books but I couldn't eat a whole one.'
Paraphrasing Barry Norman

Over to You: Self-Help Books (or just books!)

So, in the same vein as a mother who doesn't want her daughter to repeat the same mistakes she did, here are my top tips when choosing and using the genre of self-help guides:

1. **Avoid any book that promises miracles on its cover.** It won't work. You will be left feeling frustrated, let down and out of pocket. There is no miracle cure. Don't waste your money on *Ten Steps to Perfect Happiness* or *De-Stress Your Life Forever*. The same goes for magazines that contain articles with similar claims. Even more so. If one book isn't going to solve your problems then a three-page article in a women's monthly certainly isn't.
2. **Try your library**. Our local library has a section called 'Books on Prescription' and is full of books recommended

by doctors. These books offer sound advice based on clinical research. You can find a list of the many books on prescription at www.readingagency.org.uk/readingwell. They are also free. If you fall in love with the book and find it is the answer to all your questions you can always buy it later. If not, you haven't lost anything by giving it a go.

3. **There are many different types of books out there.** Some books are easy to read. A perfect example would be *The Little Book of Calm* by Paul Wilson. You can read bite-size books like these even in the midst of a panic or in the depths of despair. They give a small amount of comfort when you need some kind words or confirmation that you're not the only person who's ever felt this way. At the other end of the spectrum are in-depth books that offer whole courses in cognitive behavioural therapy and the like. There is no doubt in my mind that these books work. They are also hard going, involve a great deal of time and commitment and can bring up some uncomfortable truths that not everyone is ready to deal with. I am the sort of crazy person who loves to study and some of these books feel like you are studying for a GCSE or even A level in your own psyche. I would give most of them ten out of ten for content and common sense, but you really need to be on an even keel to attempt them and you need to have the sort of analytical mind that values such an academic approach.

4. **It's OK to give up on a book.** If your mind works anything like mine you will start a book with every good intention only to get bored or disheartened by page twenty and never get any further. That's OK! Somewhere in those first few pages will be something you can take away and use. You might think, 'If only you'd worked right through to the end you'd be feeling better by now' and hence

burden yourself with more guilt. Don't worry. Try another book. Or decide books aren't for you. It really doesn't matter. You tried. That is something to celebrate. I don't think I've ever finished a self-help book; they sit gathering dust on my bookshelf because I promise myself I will go back to them one day. I know that I never will but some kernel of truth from the pages I have read will have lodged in my mind and struck a chord.

5. **It's OK to throw the book against the wall.** Unless of course it's a library book, they tend to frown on that sort of thing. As explained in tip four, you may get nothing out of a book, but also you may find that a book has tapped into some of your darkest fears and deepest insecurities. It could make you angry, sad, afraid. It could just piss you off! That's not such a bad thing. You are engaging with the book, albeit in a negative way. You are getting in touch with something deeper in yourself. I'm not saying to carry on with a book that makes you feel crap, but the road to healing isn't paved with happy thoughts and eureka moments. By disagreeing with ideas and rejecting techniques, you are building your own path to healing. (Unless you are disagreeing with and rejecting everything – then you are probably stuck in denial and need more than a book to get you out of it.)

6. **Use a notebook to create your own tailor-made self-help book.** Before I went to Brazil I bought myself a beautiful spiral-bound notebook and filled it with all my favourite sayings, quotes and messages from friends. I stuck a few photos in for good measure and, hey presto!, I have my very own self-help book for times of need. I am sure you can create a notebook that works much better than mine. Fill it with all the insight, top tips and reassurance you find on your travels through the quagmire of self-helpdom

and it will be there for you to return to throughout the rest of your life. Remember, though, not to get bogged down writing everything and anything that you read, but only the things which spring out at you as being particularly meaningful. Not everything you read is true, and even the things you read that are true for someone else may not be useful for you.

7. **The internet: friend and foe.** You can find a lot of information and support on the internet. Some of it is actually useful. Beware and choose wisely. There are charlatans all over the place wanting to get your money and prey on your vulnerability and they will use the internet to get to you. On the bright side, there are many useful sites out there and the internet is an excellent way to reach out to others in the same boat as you via forums. You never need to be alone when you have a wireless router. I personally have never got on with internet forums. I find that they tend to be a hotbed of negativity and one-upmanship. I have the same social hang-ups meeting people online as I do if I were to walk into a party in the physical realm and start chatting to people, but many people do find this a godsend. Conversely I have found Twitter a great place to find likeminded people, many who promote their blogs (including my own), which can be a great way to share tips and encouragement.

8. **Sometimes the best self-help books aren't self-help books at all**. For all the time, energy and financial resources I've spent on the self-help genre over the years, the books that have helped me the most have not been intended for that purpose at all. Nothing can beat the escapism of a thrilling page-turner, and a novel with well-crafted characters can teach you more about life and yourself than any amount of theory. Not to mention the fact that, when you

are low (and even when you are not), a good story is easier to read than a book full of ideas. Poetry is another great way to enrich your soul; many poets found their creativity in times of despair and depression. A book can take you away from your current troubles; it can alter your state of mind and can introduce you to others who have travelled your road before. There are books of every kind out there to suit every taste and interest. The website I mentioned earlier (www.readingagency.org.uk/readingwell) also has a section on mood-boosting books, which aren't part of the self-help genre but have been recommended as giving a lift to your spirits. I can't recommend reading highly enough as a way through negative emotions. Find time to read. Find something to read. Find a quiet space to read and then, well, just read… and enjoy!

'Books are the quietest and most constant of friends; they are the most accessible and wisest of counselors, and the most patient of teachers.'

Charles William Eliot

* * *

There is a beautiful but little known book called *Hinds' Feet on High Places* by Hannah Hurnard, which I have read several times and get something new out of each time. The book is an allegory of a life journey. At the beginning the central character Much Afraid (oh how I identify with Much Afraid) reluctantly begins her journey but is given two companions to help and guide her en route. When Much Afraid sees her new companions she shrinks back in fear. The two women who are to guide her are silent and dark veils hide their faces, but Much Afraid is told they are the best teachers and guides she can have. Much Afraid isn't convinced and when she is introduced to them she shrinks in dread for the names of the two women are Suffering and Sorrow.

At first Much Afraid refuses to travel with them. She shakes in terror and asks instead if she can have Joy and Peace to journey alongside. Sorrow and Suffering seem like the two most terrifying things that she can contemplate, but she has no choice so, with fear and trepidation, she begins her journey.

Skip to the end of the book and Much Afraid arrives at her destination. Throughout the journey Suffering and Sorrow have stuck by her and patiently taught her all she needs to know to get around every obstacle she meets. They have helped her fight her demons, been there when she cried and now that Much Afraid has come to value them, she longs to have them stay with her. At the end she is reunited with her friends but they have changed (or she sees them differently?). Now they have been transformed from Sorrow and Suffering into Joy and Peace. In short, what Much Afraid had been most afraid of became the very things she had always craved.

I cry just about every time I read that passage, but they are good tears. We can't see it when we are travelling so close to sorrow and suffering, but these are the companions that can bring us to joy and peace. I'm still not there yet, maybe even my Brazilian friends aren't there yet, although they are definitely closer than me, but I remind myself that no sadness, no fear, no panic attack, no depressing duvet day is ever wasted. Quite the contrary: although these days may not help us reach our material and superficial goals, they are, in fact, the moments that matter most of all.

So I went back to Brazil for a second summer. Not so arrogant this time to think that I had anything to give but to recreate some of the amazing experiences of the year before and to renew old acquaintances. São Paulo was just the same. My team were lovely. People opened up their homes to us, gave us food they couldn't afford. As before, the children took great joy in simple pleasures like coloured pencils and singing songs. Their toys again would normally consist of plastic rubbish bags and their imagination, so we must have seemed like gods to them bringing books and coloured paper.

Same organisation, same place, but maybe I was different. Maybe my experience second time around was more of a journey inside myself or maybe it was just a failure of epic proportions. Midway through the trip I suffered a massive relapse of anxiety and depression. I couldn't go on, I couldn't function. I wanted to go home. No trigger, no warning, just panic, depression and self-pity. How could I feel sorry for myself when I was in a place where I had the least to feel sad about than anyone there? But as I've said before, and as I'm sure you know if you have any experience of it, anxiety and depression know neither rhyme nor reason. If I'd had a reason to be sad and afraid it would be normal, not an illness!

I returned to the guest house in a more comfortable part of the city, which was available to the group for respite, and I hid. I tortured myself with voices of guilt. I embarrassed myself with tears. I wrote copious amounts on my blog that I guess no one read. I was no use to anyone. In the place where twelve months earlier I had been floating high above the heavens I now plummeted down to earth with a thud.

And therein lies the journey we call life, or which I now call the Life Less Lived. In the moments I spend crying and hiding, I'm not loving it at all. Only in hindsight can I see their value, when the memory of the agony has passed. One minute we are on top of the world, the next we are wading through the Slough of Despond, desperate for any glimmer of hope to keep us from sinking. But the great truth is that in the Life Less Lived both experiences are as valid and valuable. One can bring time to laugh and celebrate, the other gives us time to rest and reflect and can bring a slow kind of hard-won healing. One gives us strength to inspire and nourish, the other gives us humility to receive support from others.

I celebrate the long road of healing, I rejoice in the Life Less Lived. I will never be as wonderful and faithful as the people I met in São Paulo but I'm on the right road, as broken, twisted and frustrating as it is. I would never go back. I am forever grateful for the things, places and people I would have missed if my pleas for a miracle cure had been answered in the way I wanted.

CHAPTER SEVEN

Accept Who you Are but Believe Who you One Day Might Be

It was late Saturday afternoon in 2009 and I needed something from the large retail park five minutes from my home. Many people have never heard of the small town where I live, but if I say I live near IKEA they all know where I mean. This time it was a simple trip to the Boots on the same park, just to get some ibuprofen and a bottle of bubble bath. It should have only taken me five minutes but three hours later, after a trip to the emergency medical centre and a double dose of diazepam, I had plummeted yet again from semi-successful career woman to the isolated depths of desolation and despair.

Since my summers in Brazil I had swung backwards and forwards between success and failure. I stuck to teaching for five years in total, the most enjoyable years of which had been teaching primary-school children. Even that came with its range of panic attacks and time off sick. I finally quit teaching after I yet again took a step too far and thought it would be a good idea to teach vulnerable teenagers who had been excluded from every sort of mainstream education imaginable. I'm not sure the kids learned much from me. I learned a lot from them, about electronic police tags, self-harm, drugs – and always locking away sharp objects and having eyes in the back of your head! I lasted about a year in that job before lying on the floor in the toilets sobbing and leaving with an anxiety sick note never to return to that job – or to teaching. Like I say, teachers have my greatest respect and admiration.

That weekend I had been working for about a year in a job that was predominantly home-based and with a team who were as diverse as they were supportive. I had plenty of things on my mind but, just as with about every other time I've crashed and burned, I was in definite denial about my anxiety. I was cured! I was absolutely one hundred per cent cured! After fifteen years I was finally better. OK, so I still took medication, but I told myself I didn't really need it. I had been through many ups and downs with my mental health but I was now in a stable place. OK, so I was still fragile, but I was working full-time for a company that knew all about my medical history and were supportive of it. I had been living in the same house for six years, was back 'home' in Nottingham and had a much better understanding of my condition. I was convinced that I was fully recovered. True, it had been only just over a year since my last period of sick leave, but it was teaching that had caused that! That wasn't me! I wasn't weak and fragile!

I pulled into the car park ready to make a dash into Boots and out again, home in time for a quiet evening in alone, my favourite way to spend a Saturday night. There were plenty of spaces in the car park and I was only going to be five minutes. I pulled into a space and started to get out of the car just as a young man with his girlfriend pulled up next to me, music booming out of the car stereo notifying everyone of his arrival.

'Oi, can't you park properly, you dozy cow?' he said to me, and strutted off to the shops, testosterone and girlfriend in tow.

I froze.

I felt sick.

I looked and sure enough I had strayed probably about six inches over the white line. It didn't really matter, the car park was less than half full, but it mattered to me.

There is no logic as to why a comment from a random, cruel and pedantic stranger caused me to collapse on that particular day, at that particular point in space and time. Maybe there was a cosmological reason why our paths crossed and events unfolded as they did. Maybe I'm just kidding to convince myself that there was some beneficial rhyme or reason to what happened next.

At the time I couldn't think at all let alone philosophise. My whole world became that young lad and the white line I had breached. Nothing else mattered, or had ever mattered or would matter again. The whole universe fell apart because I couldn't park properly. My ineptitude at parking was all the evidence I needed that I had no place in a civilised society, that I shouldn't be allowed out in public and that I was worse than useless.

I got back in the car, closed the door and did the only thing I could do. I screamed. I screamed loudly.

I screamed

I yelled

I shrieked

I screeched

I roared

I bellowed

… and I couldn't stop.

Time skipped a beat. It only felt like a few seconds that I sat there screaming, but when I looked at the clock forty-five minutes had passed. People must have come and gone past my car. My young nemesis and his girlfriend must have returned and left the scene. How nobody called the police I will never know. If they had I would surely have been sectioned. My carefully repaired and so, so fragile life had crumbled again into a thousand pieces. I was Humpty Dumpty and no number of king's horses or king's men would ever be able to put me together again.

* * *

I am an anxious person, I have a debilitating mental condition and, like a pendulum, I swing from health to disorder at frequent intervals. I accept this and, difficult as it might be to understand, I celebrate it. However, this has not always been the case. For many years, up to and including that incident in 2009, I was determined that this was not the person I wanted to be. In order to prove to anyone who would listen that I was well, I pushed myself to more and more ridiculously adventurous and outrageous extremes. Not only did I take a ten-week camping trek around America, I also travelled to Brazil to work in the favelas, where gun-toting gangs ruled the streets and drugs, diseases and abject poverty were the norm. I did this not once but twice, as if my first trip wasn't proof enough. I recovered from many months unable to work and in receipt of benefits only to train as a teacher two years later. No simple or stress-free job for me, oh no! I wanted to prove I could do anything I set my mind to. Not even teaching cute and receptive seven-year-olds, no not me. I wanted to teach teenagers! I wanted to stand in front of a class of fifteen-year-olds with no interest in science and arm them with Bunsen burner flames and hydrochloric acid just to show what I could achieve.

My life is a pendulum. It swings to and fro. I guess life is like that for everyone, but consider a pendulum. If you want it to stop swinging you have to let it run its course. Eventually it will lose momentum and come to equilibrium. I would never accept the pendulum of my life. I tried with every atom in my body to hold it on the 'healthy' side of the swing, but that takes a huge amount of energy, it goes against the status quo, it fights the natural compulsion of the pendulum (if this were a science lesson I would talk about potential and kinetic energy, but suffice to say it was exhausting to my mind and body to try and maintain this position). It was also counter-productive. Inevitably, I would let go of the pendulum, and what does a pendulum do when it has been held to one side? It swings more wildly and further than it would have if it had been left alone. From exhilarating highs to all-encompassing lows my life has been nothing if not interesting.

* * *

Back in the IKEA car park the minutes of my life were ticking by but I was paralysed in a stationary car-shaped bubble of fear. My screams eventually gave way to desperate sobs; I was utterly lost. I had some vague knowledge that I was in a car park and that I should try and get myself home, but driving was out of the question. I was only aware that I was very scared, very alone and in desperate need of the toilet!

Back in the very first chapter of this book I talked about angels. In all my experiences there has always been some kind person, some angel in human clothing, who has performed a very simple act of random kindness and has eased me back just a few inches away from the cliff-edge of insanity. I never remember anything about them, about their words or clothes, just the fact that there is kindness in a stranger can be enough. That Saturday afternoon an angel knocked on my car window. My fickle memory can't recall her age, demeanour or facial features. I remembered she asked if I was OK.

In that split second I registered that somebody cared if I was OK. A split second was just about enough to challenge my belief that everyone thought I was a freak with the parking skills of an ape.

She said something about did I have someone I could call.

This weakly penetrated my downward spiral and was sufficient to make me realise that, even though I couldn't work out how to get out of this situation myself, there might be someone I could call for help.

And then my angel disappeared. Maybe she was raptured up to the Promised Land. More likely she hurried off to buy a flat-packed shelving unit slightly embarrassed and irked by the crazy woman encounter she had just had.

I urge you, if you are ever in an IKEA car park and you see a wild woman crying and screaming in her car, please pluck up the courage to knock on the window and smile. You may feel inadequate and ill-equipped. She may shoo away your help, but years later she will remember your compassion and what it meant to her on that day.

* * *

When I look back on my life, illogical as it may seem, it is the 'IKEA moments' that I celebrate the most. Don't get me wrong, I love the many quiet evenings I have spent on the sofa reading a novel, or walking along the sea front at Whitby, or drinking over-priced coffee in a boutique café in London. Those are the times that have restored my soul and re-established my sanity, but it is the 'IKEA moments' that have developed me into the person I am proud to be today.

For many months after I crash and burn I am always ashamed and mortified. Especially when it is so public and inglorious as it was that weekend. I make excuses, I play it down, I go into denial and make light of it. Even if it happened now I would probably do the same. It's hard to be thankful for who you are when you are screaming, crying and wanting to end your life, but taking a bird's eye view of my life I claim the 'IKEA moments' as my victories, my 'I made it through the rain' days. Seen from the safe distance of hindsight I can rationalise that these are the very moments that made me strong. I may, at times, be weak and fearful, but I know what it is like to fight back from the brink of suicidal despair time and time again and come back each time wiser and gentler for it.

Tips from my Toolbox: Acceptance

This is a bitter pill to swallow, but the truth is I will always be anxious, worried and sensitive to the moods of those around me. I have battled with this fact for over forty years, not wanting to admit the truth – even now as I'm writing, a part of me still wants to scream and shout 'No, that's not really me! I am really a confident and successful person! I will one day find the secret to relaxation and inner contentment! Why would anyone want to accept worry and stress as way of life?'

Let me give you a scenario – an amalgam of many real occasions that have plagued me over the years. I am in the Peak District, miles from any town or city with the people I love most in the world. The sun is pleasantly beating down on us, all we can see for miles are hills and greenery, a few sheep and the odd stone farmhouse. We are healthy and comfortable in each other's company. I have nowhere better to be, no work to focus on, no family members in crisis or needing my help. Everything is all right with the world. Bliss!

Except it isn't blissful. The background could be different each time (a country walk, a Mediterranean holiday, a family Christmas, a relaxing Sunday afternoon at home), but the reality for me is always the same. Whenever I 'should' be relaxing my stomach is churning, my shoulders and chest are tense. In addition, there is a constant Twitter feed of worries flicking through my head. As I bat each one away another takes its place:

Why did she look at me funny? #paranoia

Did I lock the car properly? #checkeditseventeentimesalready

What's that lump in my throat? #healthscare

Why hasn't my companion spoken for the last two minutes? #doesntheloveme?

Did I file that report properly at work? #betterringandcheck

Why did I say that to Sally earlier? #embarrassing

I can't believe I say such embarrassing things! #stupid

I'm not worrying? Why aren't I worrying? I know there is something really important I need to worry about! #addictedtoworry!

For years my reaction to this was to fight it with an inner verbal dialogue: 'You idiot! Why can't you just relax like a normal person? You're ruining everything! You're ruining your whole life. You should be calm now, so calm down. Stop worrying. You ought to have got over this by now.'

And so on and so on. The result being that my stomach became tighter, my shoulders more hunched, my head began to ache with the effort of trying not to worry and be relaxed and all the time the Twitter feed was getting faster and faster, louder and louder – until there didn't seem much use trying to relax at all. The reality of the undulating hills (or the Mediterranean beach or the joy of Christmas) passed me by. My whole focus was on the imaginings inside my mind, all sorts of health scares, arguments, disciplinary hearings at work or court settlements! I have been fortunate enough to visit some of the most beautiful places in the world – and unfortunate enough to have missed most of them, not because I wasn't there (in the physical sense) but because I wasn't there!

Recently I visited a museum with some friends who have teenage boys. The museum provided mini iPods as tour guides which, as well as describing the background to the exhibits, also had games and quizzes to amuse the younger museum goer. I swear that neither boy lifted his eyes from the iPod for longer than five seconds (except when lunch was on offer). They missed every single detail of the museum. OK, they might have been being educated in their own way, but they missed the experience.

I can't blame them: this is how I live my life. However, whereas the boys thoroughly enjoyed their iPod day, my eyes are glued to disasters and worries playing out on a screen in my mind. I miss the whole experience of life and I certainly don't enjoy it!

'There is no such thing as pure pleasure; some anxiety always goes with it.'

Ovid

It took me years to accept this truth about myself. Before then I wasn't even aware of how much I was missing or how much of my attention was focused away from now into the future or the past, or how ingrained into my being were the physical symptoms of anxiety. The constant feed of worries will always stream through my mind wherever I am and whatever I am doing, my body is constantly on high alert. However, I don't have to be a victim to this anymore – I don't need to get embroiled in every disastrous imaginary catastrophe my subconscious throws at me.

Recently I was thinking about this while in Madeira, sitting on a balcony overlooking the Atlantic Ocean. It was a beautiful day where I had nothing to do, nowhere to be and no need to worry about anything. I tried to slowly focus on my environment. I could hear waves crashing against the rocks below, I could see a waiter clearing coffee cups from poolside tables below, the aroma of pizza drifted up from the little Italian restaurant on the corner and (drum roll please)… I could enjoy all these things! Yes, if I had done a quick inventory of my body I was far from relaxed, yes my annoying worry factory kept reminding me of something that could go wrong/I should have done/I ought to have been thinking about, but by then, and now, I was refusing to enter into dialogue with this part of my brain – well not at times I've chosen for myself to relax, at least. I won't battle with myself to 'make' myself relax; this always has the opposite effect anyway. But by accepting that there is going to be background 'anxiety' noise to everything I do, I can leave it where it is, turn the volume down and choose to turn my focus to the sights and sounds around me.

It is easier said than done and it takes practice, but the key is to accept things the way they are and to view thoughts with gentle curiosity and let them pass through the mind rather than dwelling on them. It is about making a conscious decision about where to focus your attentions and accepting that things will never be perfect but that, even with all the imperfections, there is still plenty to smile about. It's knowing that this is the Life Less Lived but loving it anyway.

Unfortunately, that Saturday in IKEA car park I hadn't learned any of these tools!

Over to You: Acceptance

- Do you also feel tense and worried when you 'should' be relaxing? Do you have a constant Twitter feed of worries going through your head even when you are 'supposed' to be unwinding? Stop battling with who you are and never give yourself a hard time about this.
- Next time you are trying to relax, become more aware of your body and the symptoms of anxiety that are present, don't try to fight them, just accept them.
- Be aware of the thoughts in your brain. Again, don't fight them, let them pass.
- Slowly focus your attention around you at where you are NOW, not where your brain is trying to take you.
- For more guidance on this see the tip on mindfulness on page 196.
- Every day make a conscious decision to accept who and where you are now but never let it stop you believing where you one day might be.

* * *

Christians get a lot of bad press. I criticise Christians louder and longer than most. But with my mobile phone in my hand, tears streaming down my cheeks and despair in every atom of my body, I knew that the people who would drop everything on a Saturday teatime and drive ten miles on a mission of mercy were not my closest friends or even my family (although I am sure they would have done) but acquaintances I had met through the church. One desperate, pleading phone call from a hysterical woman who was old enough to know better and Gary and Moira turned off the burners under the saucepans, jumped in the car and rushed to meet me as fast as the speed limits and teatime traffic would allow.

I was still in my car when they arrived. Still crying. Thankfully the screaming had ceased but not much rationality had returned.

I once went on a course about anxiety and was told that a panic attack can only physically last for twenty minutes. I wish the leaders of that course had seen me that day. Nearly two hours after that careless comment about my parking I was still firmly in a frenetic, panic-filled state (and still in desperate need of the loo!).

I was driven to the emergency medical centre by Gary and Moira, where I was given diazepam (which was the only thing that was going to challenge the adrenalin rushing through my body) and taken home. I took more diazepam and thankfully slept until the next morning when I woke up calm but humiliated and totally depressed.

I had let go of my pendulum of sanity and it had swung with such force and ferocity that I was left reeling and devastated by its actions. I wanted to stay in my house for ever. Turn the phones off, not leave the house, quit my job. I wanted to go back to the person I had been all those years before when my mum had brought me the picture of the Golden Gate Bridge. I regretted every single step I had taken since that day out of my safe refuge of social reclusion. I was stupid and arrogant for ever thinking I could live like a normal person, or that I could hold down a job, that I could drive five minutes down the road to the chemist without a chaperone. I was a pathetic sloth. A pariah. A joke. A worthless imposter whose life should have finished long before.

Our weakest moments make us strong
Love proves itself when we don't belong
Hope begins when we can't go on…

From *'The OK Song'*
by Gail Marie Lockwood

It has taken many years, far too many years, to accept what most people take for granted. I am a holistic person made up of many parts, some good, some disastrous. Finally I have accepted that I have my weaknesses AND my strengths. I no longer need to live life on a pendulum swinging back and forth from success to despair, but I can, with care and practice, live in equilibrium and accept both polar opposites as part of my being.

I am tenacious and very often brave. I have travelled far and wide and succeeded in as many things as I have failed at. I can teach – although it is wise for me to decide that daily teaching in a secondary school is not for me. I can write – all the better for the experiences life has sent me. I can, time and time and time again, recover from fears and depressions so horrifying that many people will never even come close to or be able to imagine. I am terribly and hopelessly weak. I scream in car parks, I run away from day-to-day encounters, I see disaster lurking around every corner, but I never, ever give in. However many times I threaten to, or promise to, or seem to, I have NEVER and will

NEVER cease to pick up the crumbled bricks of my life and start building again.

I have learned that in order to love the Life Less Lived I need to keep a balance between my strengths and weaknesses. I can't live in constant fear of another debilitation or bout of depression but neither can I deny that these are a very real part of my persona. In the same way that I need to accept that no relaxing or tranquil moment is ever going to be free from worry or the physical symptoms of tension, so I need to accept that I will never be fully cured of my anxiety disorders, and that that is no bad thing.

I needed to stop battling, stop holding tight to the pendulum and start accepting, start letting go.

I needed to see each victory as part of my journey, not the end of it.

I needed to see each 'disaster' as a wake-up call, a learning experience, a 'note-to-self' to redress some imbalance; it is not the end of life as I know it. Good times WILL come again.

You see when we really learn to love the Life Less Lived we realise it's OK to be weak. It's OK to make mistakes. For the longest time I believed I had to be strong and perfect and so each collapse came as a bitter defeat. Now I accept myself with all my serotonin imbalances, screaming heebie-jeebie fits and slough of despondency days. I am not a bad person – I am a whole person.

So, what if I'd accepted myself all those years ago on that council estate in Bristol? Am I saying that I should have accepted my lot in life in those dark days and stayed hidden behind a locked door? Was I wrong to travel to the Golden Gate Bridge? Was it foolish to train to be secondary-school teacher? Were my trips to Brazil ridiculous attempts to be someone I'm not?

Not at all. Every experience in my life has brought me to where I am today and each anecdote I tell expresses something of my personality. I am every bit the person who achieved her dreams in The City by the Bay as I am the girl who screamed herself silly in a car park three miles from her home. I am a qualified teacher – no one can take that away from me, and somehow I possibly even did a small amount of good in the poorest part of São Paulo, yet there are still days when I struggle to get out of bed, let alone travel halfway across the earth.

My battle has taken me to places I could only have ever dreamed of, so do I regret it? Do I wish I had given up the fight before it had begun? Absolutely not! All I really regret is not doing these things with the wisdom I have now and the knowledge that I need support, space and patience with myself to get things done.

I recently heard a story of a woman in her eighties who wanted to do a sky dive and thanks to her persistence and the encouragement of the people around her in the retirement home she lived in she achieved her dream. There are many people who would have said she was crazy. Many 'carers' would have said the risk was too great, that she might have a heart attack, she could break a bone; any number of potential pitfalls made this a perilous adventure. Yet why shouldn't an eighty-year-old do a sky dive any more than a twenty-year-old? I don't know but I'm guessing that the woman had to think a little more carefully about what she was doing, needed a little more help, had to push a lot harder to make her dream a reality, but she did it. I'm guessing several pages of risk assessments were filled out by the people responsible for her wellbeing, but at the end of the day, why shouldn't an adult, with all her faculties, who understands the dangers, achieve whatever she wants?

The difference between me now and the younger me is really a question of perception. If I had my time again I would still have all the same crazy adventures; I would just have 'risk-assessed' them better. Instead of rushing headlong into a foolhardy scheme with no thought to my anxiety because I lied to myself and anyone who would listen that I was 'over all that now,' I would have looked at what I wanted to achieve in the light of the person I know I am and put measures in place to protect myself from dramatic pendulum swings. I would have been kinder to myself, more accepting, more human.

* * *

How I recovered and rebounded in the days after the car park incident was my first taste of this new attitude, although it has probably taken me another six years to embrace this fully.

Alone on that Sunday, still dosed up on diazepam, I was convinced I wasn't going back to work – ever. I'm not certain of all the small knives of anxiety that had been stalking me that weekend, but I know that I was worrying about a particular situation at work. From the tone of one email received late on that Friday afternoon I had convinced myself that our manager was angry with me. That perception from one email, that I was not able to clarify or confirm until the Monday morning, had played over and over, louder and louder in my imagination until, along with a million other worries clamouring for my attention, it had exploded into cries and screams loud enough to wake the dead.

It was such a small inconsequential thing. It meant nothing. Just like the lad who criticised my parking had no intention of causing me distress. The disasters and monsters and never-ending hell-filled scenarios existed only within my mind. My mind! The one place I can never escape from.

I didn't have the manager's personal number, so that Sunday afternoon I rang one of the team leaders, ostensibly to tell her I was going off sick and would probably never be fit to return.

As I said before, they knew all about my history. They understood – well, as much as anyone can understand the irrational workings of another person's being. The team leader listened. She *really* listened. I was expecting… I don't know what I was expecting? Maybe criticism? Maybe to be told to pull myself together? I'd certainly had that reaction many times before in similar situations.

She said, 'You know I think this is partly our fault, I don't think we've given you enough support for your anxiety.'

What? That stopped me in my tracks. That wasn't the way this had played out numerous times before when I'd been forced to leave jobs.

'Please will you come and see Steve tomorrow and we'll see what we can put in place to try and stop something like this happening again?'

'What – no, I can't – I can't face anyone – ever! Especially not Steve (Steve being the manager who I had now become so afraid of).'

'It doesn't matter if you cry or don't know what to say, and you can have someone with you. No one is cross with you but please try and come and meet him and I think you will be very surprised by his understanding.'

For all the negative things I may have to say about medication I am sure it was only diazepam that got me through the next night and day and gave me the calmness and courage to attend that meeting.

We met in a pub garden (less intimidating than an office) and I dragged along a poor unsuspecting colleague as my support. Little did I know then that she had her own journey with depression, but then how little do we know of the struggles going on for any of the people we see every day?

Just as my colleague predicted, Steve was as understanding and supportive as any manager has ever been towards me. Never once was it suggested that I did less of a job, or was any weaker than any other member of my team, but based on that meeting we obtained funding for me to employ a support worker to help me through some of the more trying parts of my job. My managers gained more of an understanding of the sort of things which trigger my anxiety, things they could do to help and what I could do to help myself. One small example – I freak out if I get a voicemail from a manager that says, 'I need to talk to you – please call me back.' Before the message is finished I am imagining all sorts of scenarios involving disputes and complaints and me getting the sack. After that meeting the managers understood it was easier for me to hear, 'Can you give me a call about the Simpson contract, they need to revise their budget.' Just giving me that little bit more information meant that my imagination had no room for manoeuvre. That wasn't the last panic or upset I experienced with that team but it was the worst one, because I knew after that, however low I got, the team were, for the most part, wanting to support me and willing me to succeed.

Tips from my Toolbox: Cognitive Behavioural Therapy (CBT)

One of the results of my infamous and ignominious 'IKEA moment' was that my GP referred me for cognitive behavioural therapy. However, the course of the Life Less Lived never runs smoothly and my first visit to a CBT practitioner was an unmitigated disaster! CBT is generally hard work and takes a lot of effort and stepping out of comfort zones, but I don't think your first experience is supposed to be as calamitous as mine was!

It had taken me a while to get referred for therapy. My GP at first got me to read about CBT and research the practice on websites. While this was interesting and informative it had no impact on my levels of panic and anxiety whatsoever. When I was referred to a real live human being I found that I had been invited to a group therapy session. A GROUP therapy session, and me with a diagnosis of social phobia? Were they kidding?

I dutifully went along but the sessions were a forty-five-minute drive away in a part of Nottinghamshire that I was unfamiliar with. It turns out my satnav was unfamiliar with the area as well! After heading down blind alleys and several U-turns followed by a frustrating search for car parking I arrived. Late! Already anxious and panicky at the thought of attending the session my adrenalin levels had been piqued by the desperate drive. 'At least I'm here now,' I thought woefully. Although a large part of me wanted to head home, I decided no one would notice li'l ol' me sneaking in at the back of class – all would be well.

Or not! As soon as I opened the door I realised that, in a supreme level of bad planning, all of the seats were facing towards the door. I was, in effect, entering stage left, with twenty-five pairs of eyes watching me creep to the nearest available seat (of course, in the middle of a row) and sink as far down into my chair as was possible.

The leader/practitioner person continued her talk, which was adequate but not life-changing. It focused on what happens in the body when we have a panic attack. I already knew what happened in the body during a panic attack, not only had I lived it nearly every day of my life and taught all about the fight or flight urge as a science teacher, I had just spent weeks and weeks doing GP-prescribed homework, reading up on exactly that thing. What I wanted to know was how to stop it!

During that session the leader announced that it was reassuring to note that a panic attack cannot ever last more than twenty minutes. Errr, I know for a fact that I have had hysterical, screaming panics that have lasted several hours. Twenty minutes? Which scientific expert thought that one up? Either I'm some freak of nature (unlikely) or that twenty-minute 'fact' is clearly untrue.

None of this was what made my first session a calamity. That happened after I thought my ordeal was over. I went back to my car, shattered with emotion and with the lateness of the hour, and set off for the forty-five-minute drive home. Having got no more than forty-five seconds into my journey a car screeched past me, the driver stopped, beeped, pulled down his window and shouted, 'You stupid dumb bitch! It's a one-way street!'

I was crushed. I was a failure. It was IKEA all over again. I'm not usually a bad driver but I had misread the road signs in my tiredness and stress and made a fatal error. Well it wasn't fatal this time, but it could have been. I stopped my car where it was and sobbed/screamed/cried into my steering wheel. Not quite the IKEA incident level of panic but close. I couldn't drive home, I couldn't move. I cried and cried and felt an utter and abject failure. After what was definitely more than twenty minutes I was still no calmer and still in no fit state to drive. I could console myself with the knowledge of what was happening to my body (which was no consolation at all) or I could go and get help.

I walked back into the classroom for the second time that night. The two leaders were packing up. I think they had lots of qualifications and 'ologies'; I'm not sure how much experience they had of a middle-aged woman hyperventilating, crying and saying, 'I want to go home' over and over again!

That I got home safely that night was an achievement. That I went back four more times to complete the five-week course is quite unbelievable. I'm not really sure why I did it. Maybe because in their slightly inept and embarrassed way the tutors were kind to me, or maybe because I knew I couldn't go back to my GP and tell him it hadn't worked if I hadn't really given it a try.

The rest of the course did move onto tactics for conquering panic and anxiety but nothing that I hadn't already read about or tried. Useful tips like controlled breathing and rating your anxiety/panic on a level of one to ten and continuing to rate it as you watch the panic subside. It was a useful academic exercise and a positive test that I could actually stick at something, if only for five weeks, but it didn't really impact on my life, or my anxiety, in any way.

At the end of the course I had a chat with the tutor. This was the first time I'd had any one-to-one contact. We chatted briefly for about twenty minutes after which the tutor concluded that I had 'deep-seated core belief issues' and would need to be referred for one-to-one CBT counselling.

Huh?

Deep-seated core belief issues? What did that mean when it was at home? I mean, yes, I could have told them months before that I needed one-to-one support but I had never even heard of deep-seated core belief issues let alone even considered that I had them. I had no idea what she meant. Didn't I have enough to worry about without tormenting myself about my deep-seated core belief issues as well?

As is typical of the vagaries of the NHS I had to wait nearly a year to see anyone else or even begin to understand and address these underlying causes of my anxiety. When I did it was the single most powerful tool I have ever used to deal with my issues. It hasn't cured me, but I can quite honestly say it has changed my life and has given me a semblance of power over moods, which, for the most part, allows me to lead a relatively normal life and to achieve many of the aims that had been unthinkable to me.

So what is it all about?

There are a gazillion books out there on CBT, all written by experts in the field, most very good and useful (although I would propose not a substitute for meetings with a competent CBT therapist). I can't tell you all about CBT and what it can do for you in the space of one chapter. For a start, I don't really know, there is much more to it than I have ever experienced. All I can tell you is what I learned from the process and how it has improved my life.

My therapist Wanda was wonderful. I burst into her therapy room several months after the anxiety course and announced to Wonderful Wanda that I had deep-seated core belief issues, that I didn't know what that meant but I was sure it was really bad! Disastrous even!

Wanda took the time to explain and over the next twelve weeks we worked on my low self-esteem using a process of experimentation and challenging my negative thinking.

However I explain this it's not going to come across as well as those gazillion books I referred to earlier, but basically some time somewhere deep in the depths of my early life I developed some beliefs about myself, about the world and my place in it. We all do this. Some of us get healthy beliefs; I guess a large proportion of us aquire negative beliefs. My beliefs, for example, my 'deep-seated core beliefs' were that I am useless, ugly and unlovable.

I probably should add a caveat at this point that CBT therapy is not for the faint-hearted! First you have to look deep within yourself and acknowledge what's happening in the murky depths of your soul. That part is bad enough. You then have to challenge those beliefs by experimentation, hard work and giving yourself a good talking to! I should also add that it needs a level of cognitive ability that, without being condescending, not everyone in society possesses. Don't get me wrong: you don't need to be clever or educated, but you do need to be able, with support, to analyse your thoughts and see the error in them.

Not so long ago I met a woman who had also been sent for CBT. I was just about to wax lyrical about how fantastically effective it was when she cut me dead. 'I hated it,' she spat. They wanted me to face the things I have a phobia about – where's the point in that?'

Mmm, you can see her point, can't you? Yes I had to face some hard truths, yes I had to face some situations I was petrified of, but with Wanda's support it didn't really seem so bad.

So back to those pesky core beliefs: we have these beliefs deep in our being that we may or may not be aware of and we know they are not good, so we make 'rules for living' which keep those beliefs hidden. Our 'rules' do a pretty good job most of the time (for most of us anyway). Yet these beliefs are so fundamentally part of our psyche that they can't stay hidden forever: they keep emerging at the most inconvenient and terrifying moments. When our rules are under threat of being broken we become anxious and panicky; when we know our rules are broken we get depressed.

Confused? Let me share my rules with you, it might make things clearer. Remember my core beliefs were that I am ugly, useless and unlovable. That's a huge burden to carry around day in, day out, so somehow my subconscious made up rules that protected me from these facts. Examples of the rules I set for myself without even knowing it are:

- I must keep everyone happy
- I must not make mistakes
- I must not let anyone get cross or disagree with me

If everyone was happy and no one was cross with me and I never made a mistake I could kid myself that I wasn't a useless failure. If I thought I might have upset someone (for example, if a passer-by scowled at me or a shopkeeper snapped at me) then I was overwhelmed by a conviction of my uselessness. I could go from normal to depressed in a matter of seconds. It didn't matter that the person was a complete stranger, it was the universe that was sending me this message: the whole world was in existence to send me the message that I'm a good-for-nothing waste of space.

Even if my rules weren't actually broken I could tie myself in knots by worrying that they might be. I could do a piece of work and check and re-check and get someone else to check it. Then check it again. I would still go home and obsess that it contained a mistake. I believed that the world would end if that work had even as much as one small typing error. I didn't know why I felt like this, but then I didn't know about my rules. I could fret and stress for hours about whether I had upset some-one by my actions or even just by being – no wonder I would explode in panic or hysteria at regular intervals! Do you know how hard it is to never make a mistake, keep everyone in the world happy and make sure everyone agrees with you? It's ex-hausting! I could get anxious even if people were disagreeing on a television discussion programme. People in a studio a hundred miles away could threaten my rules because they were disagreeing.

The rules sound ridiculous now I've written them down, but that was half the battle with the therapy, learning what my rules were, naming and shaming them if you like. Of course they are impossible to maintain. I might sound like a fool but you need to understand that before my sessions with Wanda I didn't know I had these rules.

The second half of the battle was challenging those beliefs and re-writing the rule book. That's where the experimental exposure bit comes in.

'Nothing in life is to be feared, it is only to be understood.'
Marie Curie

At the time of my therapy we had a monthly team meeting at work. It was my worst nightmare. It lasted all day and was in an airless room with no natural light. There were about twenty people around a table, many with very strong personalities and vociferous points of view. It was often very tense. I actually had a support worker funded by the DWP's Access to Work Scheme to help me cope with these meetings among other things. The meetings were held on a Tuesday and the anxiety would start to build around the Thursday or Friday of the week before. My weekend before these meetings was always a washout. I spent all my energy keeping my anxiety at bay so that I could at least turn up to the meeting. I never slept very well the night before. I imagined (and dreamed of) all sorts of scenarios which involved people shouting at me and me saying something stupid. By the time I entered the room on the Tuesday morning I was a moronic wreck. Everything in my body language said I didn't want to be there. I avoided eye contact, avoided making small talk with my colleagues, sat as close as I could to the door, tried to curl myself up into an invisible ball.

Often I would have to leave the meeting to calm down. Somehow I always managed to get through it. Every Tuesday morning I used to turn my bed covers over and leave my pyjamas on my pillow. I would get home around 5.30 p.m. on the Tuesday evening and go straight to bed. My reward for making it through the meeting without handing my notice in!

Wanda and I focused on these meetings as a way of addressing my low self-esteem and rules for living. CBT is very much a tool and you need training in how to use it. And once you've used it on one job (the team meeting) you will probably need it again to work on another situation, but with practice and patience you get better at doing it automatically. You need to get the manual out less and less.

Wanda asked me what it was about the team meetings that I so feared.

'Er, someone might disagree with me, someone might shout at me, I might upset someone, I might have a different point of view to someone, someone might not like me for something I say, I might make a mistake and say something stupid.' (Der!)

'And what would happen if they did?' Wanda asked, not so helpfully.

'The world would end – obviously!'

Wanda showed me about thinking errors and we used a worksheet to carefully scrutinise what I thought was going to happen and how I could possibly approach it with a different point of view.

Then she packed me off to the team meeting to 'experiment' and report back.

Like I say, it takes time, repetition and patience. I didn't walk into that next team meeting surrounded by a serene aura of calm. I didn't expound witty rhetoric that stunned my critics into silence. I didn't run down the street afterwards with a shout of eureka. I did, however, become more aware of my thinking and how it was affecting my feelings. I did take teensy-weensy steps out of my comfort zone and – stop press! – the world didn't end.

Slowly, with Wanda's help, I learned how to face my fears. I (literally) rewrote my rules, and for a few weeks I had them written everywhere so I could remind myself of them.

My new rules are:

- I will allow people to experience a range of negative emotions.
- I will allow people to disagree with me, get angry if I make a mistake or even dislike me.
- I will allow myself to make mistakes.
- If any of the above happens, I am still a good person. I don't need to worry. The world won't end.

Do I always follow them? Do I heck as like. Do I often fall into the trap of my old rules and core beliefs? Of course. Like I say, I'm not cured – but I am much better. This is no quick-fix solution and I still have to revert to my worksheets when things get tough, but I am kinder to myself, more aware of my triggers and more able to challenge those pesky deep-seated core belief issues!

Over to You: Cognitive Behavioural Therapy (CBT)

- For CBT to work you need to be ready to face your subconscious thoughts and beliefs and have the courage to challenge them. It takes practice and repetition but it can be hugely rewarding and beneficial.
- You can find out a great deal about cognitive behavioural therapy on the internet and in your library. There is plenty of self-help material out there that is very good and which means you can start today (see reading material in the appendix).
- Like me, you may find you need the support of a one-to-one counsellor to really get the full benefits from CBT. As I write this the waiting time for CBT on the NHS in my area at least is around eighteen months (a clue that there are many people out there facing similar problems?), so it is a case of waiting or paying for a private therapist, which isn't cheap. In the UK you can use www.cbtregisteruk.com to search for a registered therapist.

* * *

I no longer work with that strong, diverse team, but only because two years later we were made redundant, and unfortunately, as you will see in the following chapter, my next manager was nowhere near as understanding. During my time there, Steve and I gave some talks to managers of a very large national organisation about what it's like to employ someone with mental health issues and the benefits it can bring to an organisation if a few small barriers are overcome and addressed. It was so empowering to talk about my condition openly in a workplace setting, not as a disaster waiting to happen but as an experience that brought insight and wisdom to my role.

I still keep in touch with many of the team, and to be honest I still cringe with embarrassment when I think about that incident in IKEA car park. Yet without it I wouldn't have accepted that around each new corner is another trial waiting to test my resolve, and I wouldn't have developed the mettle to ask for help when I need it. Better than all that, I have finally learned the lesson that accepting your weaknesses can often be your greatest strength.

CHAPTER EIGHT

Still Crazy After All These Years

I was naïve in childhood. I believed the world was a virtuous and noble place. People were either good or bad, strong or weak, friend or foe, and the bad, weak foes were kept deep in the dark forests of fairyland.

I was naïve as a teenager. I had learned that the world was not so great but I believed that I could overcome its weaknesses with my own hard work, skills and personality. I could be the heroine of the fairy tales I no longer believed in. Yes there was poverty, illness, disillusionment and sheer bad luck, but they wouldn't affect me. I was clever, tough and hard-working. I would climb the greasy ladder away from such unpleasantness.

My greatest period of naïvety came in my twenties, when I was an adult and should have known better. As a child my worldview was formed by the fairy tales read to me, and as a teen I was fed success stories by my all-girls school that could only really ever tolerate overachievers. It was the eighties and I fell hook, line and sinker for the propaganda that women could *have* it all and *deserved* it all. I longed to be a high-flying business executive with large shoulder pads and a yuppie Filofax. This was the dream we were offered as we sat in cold classrooms conjugating Latin verbs and differentiating quadratic equations – it would all be worth it in the end. OK, so maybe our teachers never mentioned the power dressing or the swanky top-floor offices, maybe I got that from *Dallas* or *Dynasty*. The point is I was impressionable and can be excused for the desires of my youth. No, it was in my twenties, after my first bout of 'illness' and then the second and then the third that I truly showed how unworldly wise I was.

In my twenties I believed that, should I be unfortunate enough to get ill, I would get better, and that would be the end of it. I could beat this. It wasn't a part of me. It was a minor irritation that could be brushed away. OK, so it took longer than I expected... and illness came back, but I was determined that it would be beaten! After all, hadn't I finished my A levels and got good grades shortly after a three-month bout of pneumonia? Hadn't I completed my 1500-metre swimming badge even though the pool was waiting to close and everyone was willing me to give up just so we could all go home? Wasn't mental illness just the same? At heart I still believed the old fairy stories – bad things live in the dark forest, not in the open areas of our minds. And even if bad things did seep out into our everyday existence I could overcome them all with my intellect and strength of will.

Maybe that's why each new panic attack, each new irrational fear, each new episode of retreating from the world became more and more depressing. I wasn't the person I thought I was. The world wasn't how it was supposed to be.

* * *

Imagine life as a journey (not an original analogy I know, but stick with me). Life is supposed to be like the M1. That's what I believed when I was younger, and that's what advertisers, TV producers and life coaches would have us believe. We start off in Leeds, in a brand new vehicle. We may not all be in Jags or BMWs, maybe we're the ones in the Polo or the Lexus, but that's OK. The screen wash is full, the tyres have tread, we've checked with the traffic news and the road ahead is clear. Some of us have satnavs, automatics, cruise control, some of us don't have that luxury, but it's pretty much one straight road from Leeds to London so it's still a comfy ride. Not a race – some of us will pootle along at 65 mph in the inside lane, but that's OK. London's the place to be. That's where we headed.

I set out with everyone else and then… what happened? Well, first my engine seemed to stutter and stall. Nothing too much to worry about – I just pulled into the hard shoulder and called the AA. OK so it delayed me somewhat, several cars passed me by, even a Renault 5 and one of those old VW camper vans, but I'd soon catch up. Then it started raining, which dampened my spirits but I was still on the right road and help was on its way. Just a little hiccup.

Back on the road again and I'm settling in for the ride swiftly forgetting my short delay, then – wouldn't you believe it – I need the loo! All right, there's a service station up ahead – quick stop – fill up with petrol just in case – maybe get a coffee and some chocolate to perk me up, then back on track.

It seems I haven't been back on the road for five minutes and I see red tail-lights backing up in front of me. I apply my brakes and come to a halt in the middle lane. We haven't even got to Sheffield yet; I was hoping to be nearer to Leicester by now. After a few choice words to no one in particular I resign myself to my fate – turn the radio up and crawl forward as the minutes of my life tick by. Each minute waiting in this queue is a minute I could have been enjoying at my destination. I feel frustrated, cheated, angry, but there's nothing I can do about it.

Eventually the traffic speeds up again (with no evidence of what had caused the huge tailback – typical). I'm getting fed up with this journey. Motorways are boring! And I need the loo again! I feel sleepy as the miles tick by with only the view of grey tarmac for company, but at least I'm moving. I'm moving in the right direction.

Then disaster strikes! Nothing major like a crash or another breakdown, but we're just past Trowell service station and the matrix signs are telling me that the road ahead is closed and we will be diverted at Junction 24. DIVERTED!! Really?? Will I ever get where I'm going?

I follow the diversion round winding country lanes. The route is busy, so I take time to stop, get my map out, look for an alternative road. I should be in London by now, enjoying the successes of my journey. Relaxing. Instead I'm in a layby in Leicestershire with no idea which way I'm supposed to go. It's raining again. It's cold and it's getting dark.

And now? In my journey/life analogy? I've been wandering around these back streets for so long that I've forgotten where I'm going. I've certainly forgotten why I wanted to get there with such urgency. I've spent most of the journey cursing these delays, berating myself for my failings, jealous of those who seemed to pass along in the fast lane without a hitch.

It's only in the last couple of years that I've had the epiphany that has made me see things in a different way.

'Everything will be OK in the end. If it's not OK, it's not the end'.
John Lennon

John Lennon once said, 'Everything will be OK in the end. If it's not OK, it's not the end.' That's all very well but I have often thought, as have many people whose lives have taken an unexpected detour, 'When will it ever end?' I'm guessing you've probably thought that, too; my detours and diversions in life are all too familiar to so many people.

Was my anxiety disorder over when I reached the Golden Gate Bridge? I'd thought so at the time but then it came back to haunt me over the coming year. Was it over when I had my 'count my blessings' revelation at the site of the World Trade

Center? I'd like to tell you it was, but the fact that I'm writing this over ten years later will give you a hint that that wasn't the end of the story by any means. It wasn't even the end when I sat screaming in IKEA car park or hiding in a guest house in Brazil. I would say that all these events were stepping stones to the end but I was fooling myself all along by thinking that my anxiety and depression were something outside of me that I could fight. No, they are a part of me that can be a blessing as well as a curse but are definitely things I need to work with and not obliterate.

> 'Failures, repeated failures, are finger posts on the road to achievement. One fails forward toward success.'
>
> C S Lewis

In fact, it seems that, whenever I am finally feeling I have achieved an even keel, like I have beaten my old paranoia and fears, it is then that my old demons come back to haunt me. I have now realised that this is who I am and this journey I am on will never be over this side of eternity. I have also *finally* accepted that, far from being a noose around my neck, this 'disorder' or 'weakness' is in fact a fundamental part of myself, not to be feared, battled or got rid of, just accepted and experienced. My anxiety is the very part of me that has led me into the Life Less Lived, but it is also the thing which has made me a stronger, better person and brought me a varied, interesting and scenic life.

Take the six months prior to me starting this book. It had been around four years since my last big anxiety attack in IKEA car park. Oh yes, I'd had minor panics, upsets and irrational fears but I had found ways to manage them and keep them under control. Yes I was still on medication, but I wasn't really sure it actually did anything. I was living a reasonably normal life. Possibly not in the fast lane of the M1, but I'd certainly found an A road I could meander along quite happily. I was holding down a job, without the aid of a support worker. Then just when I think I'm winning, all the old ghosts come back to haunt me.

Tips from my Toolbox: Coping with Panic Attacks

They say that practice makes perfect. If that's true then I have definitely perfected panicking after many years and hundreds of anxiety attacks! I must be an Olympic champion by now!

Joking aside, I have, over the years, learned to understand and manage my panic attacks. I've never quite been able to eradicate them from my life completely, but for the most part I am in control of my emotions and do not let them control me.

Panic is the body's way of keeping us alive and keeping us safe from danger. Something triggers our fear and we go into fight, flight or freeze mode. Changes take place almost instantaneously in our body, hence the reason it is a physical as well as a mental experience, and can seem to come from nowhere:

- The rational part of the brain tunes out and the amygdala (the part of our brain that deals with automatic fear responses) takes over, which is great at helping us react quickly to the threat but no good at letting us think straight.
- Adrenalin is released into the blood stream and your heart beats faster to get blood to your muscles so you can make a quick exit and blood is diverted away from normal bodily processes like digestion, which is why you might feel nauseous. If you are like me you will also need to go to use the toilet! (If you are sick or empty your bowels, you are lighter and this will make it easier to run away).

- You can then start to hyperventilate which means that your body is taking in too much oxygen (although perversely, it seems like you can't get your breath).
- Your pupils will dilate to help you to better see the predator, which might lead to your vision becoming impaired.
- You might shake or feel dizzy or 'unreal'.

If these symptoms weren't bad enough then, if you are like me, you cry or scream, you almost become afraid of the fear. I learned quite early on that a panic attack isn't going to kill me; it took me much longer to realise that neither will it engulf me completely nor will it last forever.

You will be eternally grateful for your body's ability to make these changes if you are faced with an armed attacker or a wild animal or… well, any real danger. You will be able to react more quickly than you ever thought possible, you will run and fight like a gladiator. Unfortunately, for most triggers of our anxiety in the modern world we don't need our body to react in this way.

If I have a lot of work to do and a tight deadline, I imagine being shouted at because I've missed my deadline. My body reacts in exactly the same way as if a tiger walked into the office. To deal with a tiger in the office I need blood in my legs, I need an excess of oxygen; I need my amygdala to take over so I can react instinctively and quickly. To get my work done I need to think rationally, take things one step at a time and keep a professional calmness about my persona. Unfortunately, my subconscious can't make the distinction between the two threats, so it reacts to every danger as if it were a ferocious tiger.

So here are my tips for dealing with a panic attack. Even though I can't completely control them, I can reduce them from happening by probably about 90 per cent and when they do happen I can normally reduce their effect and their duration quite considerably.

Over to You: Coping with a Panic Attack

- Remember: it won't kill you and it will pass.
- Try to slow down and control your breathing. I've never found it necessary to breathe into a paper bag, which is the technique they seem to prefer on TV and movie screens, but if you can slow the intake of oxygen and increase the amount of carbon dioxide you exhale it will have a calming effect.
- Your rational mind has left the building so, if you can speak at all, you may say things that are irrational such as, 'I want to die.' I now find it helpful to have a comforting phrase which I can force myself to repeat like, 'I'm OK' or 'This will pass.'
- If you can, go for a walk or do something physical. Your body is prepared for physical activity, so even pacing up and down or rocking can help release some of the pent-up chemicals in your body.
- Don't be embarrassed! OK, so I've never quite mastered this one because people WILL look at you as if you've just arrived from Planet Zogg (especially if you are screaming and rocking!). When I was at my worst I used to carry a card with me that explained that I was having a panic attack and it would pass. It also included the number of my doctor and even a helpful website giving more information on panic attacks. Probably a little over the top! Nowadays I usually manage to say, 'I'm having a panic attack' and people tend to have enough empathy and knowledge to accept this and be sympathetic.
- Sometimes if I feel I'm unable to calm down, it helps to give my panic a mark out of ten where ten is 'screaming in IKEA car park' and one is 'chillaxing in my garden at home.' It helps to see that, although I may be far from

composed and I may still be shaking and crying, I have progressed from the screaming, wailing wreck I was thirty minutes earlier.

- In the aftermath of a panic attack self-care is vital. For a few days you will be very vulnerable and will need to sleep, rest and indulge yourself with nourishing activities. Not only has your body been through a physical shock, your mind will be torturing itself by reliving the whole sorry incident, telling you that you are back at square one and calling you all the names under the sun. It's hard to resist these negative messages when you are inevitably feeling low. Try to focus on anything positive you can take from the experience and how you can move on. It's done; it's happened; leave it in the past. Don't let this experience define your future.

If you are with someone who is having a panic or anxiety attack:

- Keep calm.
- Reassure them with simple phrases like:
  'You're OK'
  'It's just a panic attack'
  'It will pass'
  'You are safe.'
- Encourage them to breathe slowly and concentrate on their breathing.
- If possible, take them somewhere quiet where no one is staring at them.
- Give them a drink, tissues and time to recover.
- Afterwards treat them as normally as possible to reassure them it's nothing to feel embarrassed or guilty about.

* * *

Hindsight is a wonderful thing, and maybe now I can see signs that things were building to a crescendo, but at the time I just didn't spot it. In fact the day before my huge meltdown (the one where I quit my job rather than face phone calls from my manager) I had been to the cinema, laughing and joking, having a wonderful day. I had no portent of what was just around the corner.

So I'm meandering down the winding road with no major incidents on the horizon. I was able to manage all but my most severe panic attacks and felt in control of my life. I was practically 'normal'! My brother had been taken very suddenly and seriously ill a few weeks before and we had been whizzing down to London and back for visits (ironic given my earlier scenario). It was a worrying time – anyone would have found it so – receiving a call to say that my healthy, strong brother was having life-saving surgery came completely out of the blue. To rush down and find him lying in intensive care in a north London hospital having never had a day off sick in his life was heart-breaking. This experience had its effects on me, but I don't think it was the trigger. OK it made me tired and emotional, but I can usually handle the big catastrophes in life. It surprises most people that I am very calm in a crisis. Yes my dad had also been unwell, but again, nothing was dragging me down.

One thing I have learned throughout twenty years of anxiety disorder is to know my triggers. I don't always spot them in time but I know them and they are predominately to do with the workplace and my attempts at perfection.

I had been in my new job as a bookkeeper for about a year when a new manager arrived with fresh ideas and sweeping-broom changes. I was positive about this. The place needed a change. I liked him. I wanted to do well and I was very good at my job. Overqualified, enthusiastic and conscientious. My desire for perfection and attention to detail makes me a perfect bookkeeper; it also keeps me awake at night and gives me nightmares about spreadsheets that don't balance or accounts which don't reconcile.

I had twenty hours a week on the job, which might have been enough had the person one step senior to me not have been moved to head office with no thought from the powers that be of who was to take over his role (er, that would be me, then!). It might have been enough if the systems and arrears had been kept on top of before I started and didn't need a complete overhaul. It might have been enough if it hadn't been based at a retirement village where, as well as banking and invoicing, I was expected to entertain residents at fayres, dancing contests and by wandering around the village dressed as a Mexican gnome (yes! A Mexican gnome! You read it correctly!). We even had to clean the toilets one time when the cleaner was on holiday – not normally in the job description of a bookkeeper. I didn't really mind doing this – it added variety – but mostly I couldn't fit it into my work time so ended up 'volunteering' my time for free. It was a charity so no one was going to pay me for the extra hours I did weekly and, while someone more assertive and sensible might have said no to the extra work, I was trying to please my new boss and not let my colleagues down. Being eager to please is one of my major failings – as is not being able to say no. I did 'free' overtime almost every week, which maybe didn't matter. Don't we all go above and beyond the call of duty at times?

I had never hidden my mental health history. In this day and age with pre-employment health questionnaires it is very difficult to do that even if you want to, which I don't. I always talked openly about my weaknesses, some might say too openly.

I started having panic attacks. Not too bad at first, but then I started having them at work. Well, to tell the truth I only had two in the workplace. The first one was embarrassing enough and it was clear people didn't understand although the manager tried to be supportive. He said I was allowed to have one wobble as I was a woman! Even then I didn't really heed the warning signs. What should I have done? Maybe gone to the doctor? Maybe asserted myself and said 'no' to large parts of my workload that weren't in my job description? Who knows?

It was a Tuesday morning and I was covering for someone else who was on annual leave. I had a deadline of noon to complete his part of the work, but the information I needed had not been prepared by my colleague. I also had three or four things of my own with deadlines of that day. Then the ATM cash machine broke. It was my responsibility to keep the cash machine working and the new manager made it clear it should never be out of order. I couldn't mend it. I was getting aggravation from the residents because it was broken and, even as I was at the machine trying to fix it, they were coming to me in their droves to berate me because they needed cash to buy their *Radio Times*.

I was near to tears, fully aware of the looming noon deadline and my other end-of-the-day deadlines.

I still couldn't get it fixed.

I'm not an engineer. I am a bookkeeper. I am also a people pleaser. I don't like people being angry at me.

I went into the back office and had a complete meltdown. I was crying, shaking, panicking. I kept saying 'I can't do this job,' 'I can't do this job.' I was worried about the cash machine. I was worried about the deadlines. I was worried that everyone was angry at me. I was worried that I was going crazy yet again. I felt sick and faint and wanted to tear my hair from my head. The world was ending again – everything around me seemed surreal. I wasn't sure where I was or what I was doing – I just knew I couldn't do it. All I could do was cry and shake and panic.

The assistant manager was understanding and sent me home. Having left so many jobs through anxiety it always adds to my fears when something like this happens because, as well as the current experience, I pile on myself the memories of everything that has happened before. Nevertheless, after several hundred panic attacks over the years I have a better understanding of how to deal with them and I calmed down somewhat after a couple of hours at home, enough to put things into perspective. It was a bad day. I normally liked my job. I could go back the next day and maybe get some help with some of my duties. It wasn't so bad, was it? I wrote down the things I was struggling with, I reasoned with myself. The assistant manager and another colleague had been very understanding. I began to believe that things could be resolved.

Mmmm.

The new manager rang me that evening and all hope of a swift return to work crumbled.

He wasn't angry exactly, just 'disappointed', and told me I couldn't 'go off like that' at work and he would have to write a report, adding that if I 'came back the next day my job would be safe.' He didn't ask me what had happened or want to hear my side of the story. He couldn't understand why I was crying – but crying was all I could do. Panic filled my body. Before the phone conversation I had been talking myself back to normal but hearing him say 'my job would be safe' just blew my mind! My head went – I don't know where – any rational thought was gone. This conversation tipped me right over the edge. As he talked at me I fell further and further into a frozen fuzz of despair. At some point during that conversation I decided my life was over for real this time. I wanted to kill myself.

Hysterical and inconsolable I got through that night until the next day when the GP signed me off work and put me on diazepam. I was suicidal with worry. My life was over. Again. I had ruined everything. I had let everyone down. Again! I berated myself with all sorts of hateful thoughts. Rational thought left the building! I should have done more 'free' hours. I should have been able to cope with the workload. I should have been able to say no. I'd worked my hardest, put my heart and soul into the job. Never made an error or put a foot wrong and yet my job was in jeopardy if I didn't turn up for work that day. The procedure for phoning in sick was that we had to speak to the manager ourselves. I was hysterical when I came out of the doctors but I rang the manager and left a message saying I was signed off. I told him about the diazepam. Nobody who saw or heard me that day could doubt that I was genuinely very distressed and ill. In fact I remember I rang him from the pharmacy when I was collecting my diazepam and the pharmacist was very worried about letting me leave on my own. In fact it wasn't until she knew I had someone with me that she let me go. This distress must have come over to the manager but I managed to ask that he please not call back as I needed time to calm down. The very last thing that I could face was talking to a manager from work (or even any human being outside my family. Let's face it – I was a wreck).

He rang me straight back. I got in a renewed panic when I saw he had called and had to take two diazepam just to cope with the phone call. I was deep inside myself – the world was too scary to contemplate and this one manager (who probably just wanted to get his accounts completed and his cash machine fixed) in my paranoid mind represented all the evil forces in the universe.

He rang again the next day, which set off a whole new raft of fear and panic. Every time my emotions began to reach anything approaching rational it seemed he would ring. At this point my friend took over my mobile phone. I was afraid of it. I kept looking at it thinking he would ring. I felt sick to my stomach and more afraid of this stupid phone and what he might ring and say than if a lion had been at my front door baying for my blood.

Of course it isn't rational. It makes no sense. If you have any experience of panic then I hope you will understand. The manager didn't understand. He wanted answers but I couldn't give him any. All I could do was weep and hide behind my dutiful and long-suffering friend.

My friend stayed at my side day and night for several days and the manager didn't ring over the weekend. By the Monday I, fooled into thinking I was getting better after a weekend of diazepam, nipped to the local supermarket on my own. I only needed one or two bits and there was no urgency for them at all. Hadn't I learned anything from IKEA gate? Just around the dairy aisle my mobile rang. I felt sick and started to hyperventilate. I looked at the caller display. It was the manager. 'It's OK I told myself, I don't have to answer it.'

When I didn't answer it rang again, from a different number but I knew from the area code that it was still him. I hardly ever get phone calls – who else could it be? I started to cry and tried to get out of the shop (as if running away would stop the phone ringing). It didn't stop. I was shaking and sobbing. People were looking. Someone offered me a paper bag. I wanted to scream. I wanted to jump under a train. Anything, ANYTHING to stop him ringing me. How can I explain how much fear this potential phone call incited in me? It was like I was facing the executioner's blade, a devastating tsunami, the hounds of hell. Every fear, every dark force, every disastrous calamity rolled into one could not have provoked more fear than that ringing phone.

I got out the shop but couldn't make it to the car. I sat on the floor in the car park outside ASDA and wailed. I literally wailed. The phone beeped telling me I had a text. *Ring me as soon as possible* it said. He wasn't taking no for an answer.

My rational mind had completely left the building. My overriding aim was to stop these phone calls. I needed to cut off this perceived danger. I believed that my only chance of ever getting back to normality was to stop the phone ringing.

There were a hundred sensible things I could have done at that point. Ring my friend for a start. Or go for a walk. Or ring my union. Or even throw the dastardly phone in the nearest canal! I was exhausted, afraid and completely out of my mind.

I did possibly the worst thing I could have done. I rang the manager up and through sobs, moans and hysterical wails I told him I was never coming back and please, PLEASE stop ringing me.

I felt bereft, crazy, destroyed (self-destroyed). I said I was sorry I had let everyone down. He said, 'You've let yourself down' and hung up the phone.

So I was left with nothing. No job – no self-respect – no confidence to face the day – no energy left to fight another battle with my inner terrors. Just the familiar feeling of being back at square one, of letting my irrational fears beat me again (for even in the pit of my panic I could identify that I had no one but myself to blame for my demise).

Don't get me wrong, don't think I have some private income that means I don't need to work and can be a lady of leisure. I have no savings or investments, I live from pay cheque to pay cheque, I can't afford *not* to work! Yet when panic takes hold the only thing I can see is the object of my fear, that is the only thing that makes sense, that is what I need to flee from. Even living on the breadline, being repossessed or never getting another job are small matters compared to the all-consuming fear of another phone call from work. How can I ever get you to understand unless you have also been through similar fears?

Tips from my Toolbox: Guide for friends, family and colleagues

The experience highlights exactly how not to treat an employee who has mental health issues. My line manager wanted solutions, he didn't have time for tears or insecurities; he either wanted me to come back and do the job without 'throwing a wobbler' or he wanted to get someone in who would. I felt like a faulty part that either needed to be fixed or replaced. Either way, production needed to get back to full speed as soon as possible.

It's quite common for even close friends and family to want to 'fix' you and to think they know the best way to do it. I remember a time when the Golden Gate Bridge was a distant dream. I was at rock bottom, suicidal and trying to find a way out with small steps. I decided to take a few days away to stay with a very old friend – a change of scene, a chance to put things in perspective. My old friend is now an even older friend, despite the fact that she has no concept of how to support someone with mental health issues and is definitely not my first port of call if I'm struggling. My friend decided to 'help' me by telling me exactly how things were: 'You'll never get a job, you'll never find a man, you'll lose all your friends, you'll be on benefits all your life.'

My friend wasn't wrong and I know that she was trying to jolt me into some sort of action. Her intentions were good (hence why we are still friends) but her approach... well let's just say I left a day early and came home feeling more depressed, more suicidal, more hopeless and desperate than I ever was before.

Then again I could give a thousand examples of how not to do it and I do realise that it is impossible to understand if you have never experienced panic or depression. It may be impossible to understand, but it is quite possible to empathise.

So how do people like my friend Kathryn and my dad get it so right when equally well-intentioned people get it so wrong? I don't know the answer to that, but I can give you some tips overleaf if you are close to or working with someone with depression or anxiety. I also know that my dad had no concept of depression or panic attacks before I took ill... but he loved me and because of that he took time to understand and listen and come with me to psychiatric appointments; he took time to be with me, quite often in silence, and he stuck by me through thick or thin, even though it must have hurt and cost him dearly to do it.

If I have only one regret about my years of anxiety and depression, it is the effect it has had on my family and friends.

Over to You: Guide for friends, family and colleagues

- **Be gentle and kind**. The person you are supporting already has a thousand negative thoughts in their head. They will probably feel they are on the inside looking out or that it is them against the world and, even if you are related they will probably see you as one of 'them'. Shower them with kindness and compassion; it's possible they won't accept it because they feel 'unlovable', but criticism and force will just cause them to draw up the barriers even further and they will shut you out. A gentle approach will help the person to trust you and let you in.

- **Be a human being not a human doing.** If you love someone, how much do you want to fix them and make them better? You can't! There are things you can do to help them heal and the main one, after being gentle and kind, is just being. My friend Kathryn is so lovely because she gives me a place to just 'be'. After each panic or during each depressive episode Kathryn would just let me sit on her settee and play with her kids. She didn't even feel the need to talk. (I've never asked her if that's just because she didn't know what to say, but it doesn't matter – her being there was enough – she didn't need to do or say anything).

- **Listen.** Be curious, ask questions, ask about the feelings of the person you are supporting, their triggers and coping strategies, their physical symptoms. I mean to say don't bombard them incessantly with interrogations (be gentle) and take time, plenty of time, to wait for answers and then listen to the answers and take them on board. It's really OK to sit in silence and let the other person gather their thoughts.

- **Remember everyone is different.** Because I have experience of anxiety and depression, it doesn't mean I understand anyone else who has been through something similar. Recently I was having a bad weekend so I texted my friend. *I'm coming straight over* she texted back. Immediately my panic rose tenfold: *No, no, I don't want you to come over Im not in a fit state to see anyone.* Thankfully my friend listened and we met up a couple of weeks later, but it turns out she had read something that said people with depression need to be around people and not left on their own. That may be true for many people but I know myself, and I know the fastest way to recovery for me is on my own. It's easy to make assumptions about what a person needs but it's not always helpful.

- **Give signposts and suggestions rather than advice and ultimatums**. You don't know what's best for the other person; you might think you do, especially if you are a parent or spouse, but it's their life. Giving suggestions – say to visit their GP or get back to work or to take a walk – are fine but it's their decision, indeed their right, to completely ignore what you suggest. The same goes for ultimatums or home truths which, however well intentioned, are likely to backfire and it's a sure bet that the person you are talking to has already imagined far worse scenarios than you can ever propose to them.

- **Normalise but don't minimalise.** There's a fine line between explaining to someone that it's common to feel how they do (it can be helpful to know you are not alone) or to minimise the way they feel ('oh you're just feeling sorry for yourself – we all get like that'). Anecdotes can be helpful as long as you remember it's about them and not about you.

- **Be patient.** Healing is a slow process that involves going over the same ground and returning to the same spot time and time again. You might think that if the person could just get a job, get out the house, look on the bright side etc.

that everything would be all right, but it doesn't work like that. If you want to help you need to be in it for the long haul and accept setbacks and upsets as part of the process.

- **Look after yourself.** This should probably be number one on the list. Watching someone you love torture themselves is hard going. They may say things that cut you to the bone, such as telling you they want to die. You don't want to believe it so you'll reply with something like 'Don't be silly' or 'Don't talk like that,' which immediately cuts off all communication and leaves the person alone. But you are alone too and your feelings and experiences are just as valid as theirs. If the person you are trying to support is an adult with mental capacity (which you have to assume they have unless it has been proven otherwise) then you are not responsible for their emotions or actions. That doesn't mean you can't be with them every step of the way, but you don't need to feel guilty or accountable for everything they do. This is why it can be easier and possibly better, for a person who is struggling, to talk to a stranger; there is a distance between the two people and the listener isn't emotionally involved.

- **In the workplace.** There is a brilliant little booklet produced by ACAS called *Promoting positive mental health at work* that gives good advice on how to support employees who are going through difficulties. It can be downloaded from the ACAS website (www.acas.org.uk/mentalhealth). There is also an organisation called Mindful Employer (www.mindfulemployer.net), which supports organisations to be positive about mental health in the workplace.

* * *

That was three years ago and life has inevitably moved on. It took me months to recover (and in case you are wondering, my brother has recovered very well too). For a year I still flinched when the phone rang and felt sick every morning until I knew the postman had been and there was no letter from the organisation I used to work for. Mostly I feel that, yet again, I have become a victim of my own fears and failings. I feel bad about the wonderful colleagues I abandoned. I hate that I let them down so badly but was too afraid to contact them and face my own failings. I felt sick that I was back on benefits and that I had returned to the bottom of the rubbish heap from whence I came. Even though my slough of depression was more short-lived than previous episodes it still hurt. Even now I still have nightmares that I am back in that office and can't get everything done in time or everyone is shouting at me. I actually got back into work within three months with a much more supportive employer, a more interesting job with better pay and recovered much quicker because of all the experiences that had gone before and all I had learned along the way.

But why would I be glad to be going through all this again? Every time I fail, every time I fall, it is a chance to redeem and revive myself anew. It is a time to look into my soul and learn a new lesson. It hurts like hell but every single time this has happened I have always come out the other end stronger, wiser, healthier. All my life I have battled with mental illness, and it has been a battle. I have always seen it that way. Sometimes I win. Sometimes I lose. Sometimes I can trample it down and suffocate it so much that I can hide it. Sometimes it overwhelms me with an all-consuming terror. That was my final battle. Not my final anxiety attack that particular fall from grace; that was when I stopped fighting and began to accept.

Somewhere in the midst of all that craziness, when my stomach has been churned apart by worry or when I've woken up in a cold sweat after my latest nightmare, I had a small epiphany. How about I stop battling with something that is essentially a fundamental part of my existence and just experience it instead. How about I celebrate my unique journey in life and be thankful for it instead of trying to be someone I'm not. Maybe if I slowed down and enjoyed travelling the back roads, stopped trying to think in terms of success and failure but just appreciated the ride, I could learn to accept myself, my whole self, and not just the bits I liked. Maybe I could learn to love the Life Less Lived.

You probably know the famous poem by Robert Frost, 'Two Roads Diverged In a Wood'. I have loved it since I was a child. I always subconsciously wanted to be the person who *chose* the Road Less Travelled, but I never did. That would have taken guts and strength of character, which I didn't possess. Instead the Road Less Travelled chose me. I fought it and battled to get back onto the straight and narrow, but my anxiety disorder has taken me to places I would never have otherwise travelled and brought amazing people into my life who you just don't find on the motorways and A roads of life.

I shall be telling this with a sigh
Somewhere ages and ages hence:
Two roads diverged in a wood, and I,
I took the one less traveled by,
And that has made all the difference

Extract from *'Two Roads Diverged In a Wood'*,
by Robert Frost

To put it another way, the Road Less Travelled is the Life Less Lived. Especially if it chose you and you didn't intend for it to be that way. The Life Less Lived just can't happen in the fast lane. It has twists and turns, dead ends and diversions. Many breaks and stops to look at the scenery. If it's forced on you then you have a choice. You can fight the Life Less Lived or you can thank God (or whoever you are thankful to) for bringing you to a different appreciation of life. If you're living the Life Less Lived you may never get to your original destination but I bet it has made you a more resilient and judicious person. I bet you have met some amazing people, spotted some beautiful landscapes and I'm sure you have some stories to tell.

What I didn't know when I first heard this poem, at the age of fourteen when all my dreams were still intact, was that like Robert Frost I would be telling this with a smile. Somewhere ages and ages hence, two roads diverged in a wood, and I (reluctantly) took the one less travelled by, and that has made all the difference, hooray!

CHAPTER NINE

People Who Inspire: You never know how far your influence will reach

For several years I have been doing a small part-time job which involves befriending teenagers who have issues and need extra support. I only do it for a couple of hours a week and often it is difficult to know if what I'm doing is making any difference at all. You don't get many thank yous from troubled teens, you can't often see the results of your work in the same way you can in accounts when a bank account reconciles or an annual report is submitted to Companies House. Basically, you just need to have faith that the impact you are making will have a positive influence, if not now then later down the line.

At a recent team meeting where all the befrienders get together and discuss good practice, one of my colleagues (let's call her Jill to protect the innocent) was talking about a difficult link she had where the young person did not seem to be responding and Jill was feeling rather deflated that she was wasting her time. 'But I'll keep going,' she said to us. 'Who knows what I'm writing on the template of that young girl's life that she might remember later on.'

That really struck me. We all write on the template of the lives of the people who cross our paths. What do we write? Is it positive and uplifting? Or does it break people down?

Our lives are not our own. From womb to tomb, we are bound
to others. Past and present. And by each crime and every
kindness, we birth our future.

From *Cloud Atlas* by David Mitchell

I'm always fascinated by the story of Rosa Parks and how one
seemingly inconsequential action of hers sparked events that would
eventually lead to equal rights for African Americans. Rosa Parks
was just an ordinary woman. True, she was a member of NAACP
(National Association for the Advancement of Colored People) in
Montgomery, Alabama, but she didn't set out that day to start a
protest. She had had a long shift at work, she was tired and, as she
would later say, all she was doing was trying to get home from work.

Rosa caught the bus home as she had done many times before
and dutifully sat in the portion of the bus allocated to 'coloureds'.
As the bus became busier and the seats for white people became
full the bus driver moved the goal posts. He moved the sign that
separated white from black so that Rosa and three other passengers were now sitting in seats allocated to whites. The bus driver told them to get up and give their seats to white passengers.
Three of them complied. Rosa stood her ground. She refused to
move from her seat and was summarily arrested.

As soon as word of Rosa's arrest got out, NAACP planned a
boycott of the Montgomery bus service to take place on the day
of Rosa's trial. The bus boycott, which was planned for one day
only, actually lasted 381 days and only came to an end when
the US Supreme Court ruled that Montgomery's segregated bus
system was unlawful. That was by no means the end of the fight
for civil rights in America, but out of the bus boycott emerged
a prominent leader by the name of Martin Luther King Jr. who
would go on to lead a host of peaceful protests and ultimately
change attitudes and laws in one of the biggest and most influen-
tial countries in the world.

And all because a respectable, hardworking black woman became weary of being bossed around by white men and said no. Not bad for someone who was just trying to get home from work.

> 'You must never be fearful about what you are doing when it is right.'
>
> Rosa Parks

You're probably aware of the butterfly effect. In a chaotic system it is believed that minute changes in the starting conditions can have huge and unpredictable consequences. The typical example is that a butterfly flapping its wings in China can cause a hurricane to change direction several weeks later in America.

Weather is a chaotic system, which means it is impossible to predict more than a few days in advance, but there is no system more chaotic than life. I see Rosa Parks as the butterfly whose wings eventually led to a black US President. She could never have predicted the results of her actions that day; she just did what, in that moment, she felt was right. The rest, as they say, is history.

Rosa Parks is a rather extreme example of the fact that we never know how far our influence will reach or how our actions will affect others for good or bad. True, not many of us will change the course of history in such a dramatic way, but everything we do makes a difference to someone, and possibly to many someones. We really never can tell, but we can make a decision whether our influence on the world is going to be positive or negative.

Often, more often than I care to admit, I have felt weak and useless. A failure. A waste of space who makes no contribution to society. I have spent enough time on benefits to feel like a drain on the economy and even when I am working I have often felt like my contributions were meagre and ineffectual.

I will never be a Rosa Parks. I would like to discover a cure for cancer or eradicate poverty or make the world wake up to ending wars and persecutions but it's pretty likely that will never happen. I do know now that that doesn't make me useless. I gave up teaching because it was more than I could cope with, but does that mean I've never had a positive influence on a child? I spent only a short time in the favelas of Brazil and felt I had nothing to offer or give to the people I met but does that mean I gave nothing?

We all make a difference. You, me, the annoying person in your office or the one who takes time to stop when you're crying on the street. I am honest enough to feel ashamed of the fact that sometimes my influence has had a negative effect on people. I have no time machine to go back and change that but I can change myself for the future. And I don't have to cause massive waves. The ocean is made up of a trillion drops but each drop counts towards the ocean.

If you are a driver you will have inevitably been cut up, bibbed at or been on the receiving end of an angry gesticulation. For many years such experiences, which happen in a split second, would cause in me such a panic that I would not be able to complete my journey. I have pulled over to the side of the road in hysterics on more occasions than I can recall. At the worst depths of my illness I could not even venture out in the car, not because I have any phobia of motorways or traffic congestion, but because I just could not cope with the effect other drivers had on me. I am a good driver. I always have been, but one of my coping strategies is to stick religiously to the laws of the highway to avoid antagonising anyone. Ironically, the angry drivers are usually the ones who are in the process of committing a minor traffic offence. They justify their actions by bullying their way around the streets. Even now, such road hogs cause my heart to race and the panic to rise, but I have developed the tools to breathe, relax and carry on without too much interruption to my day. In the past it could have taken me a week to recover.

But what of Mr Angry? How did the rest of *his* day go? Did he have to cancel his plans because our paths crossed? I very much doubt it. I very much doubt he had any concept of the level of distress he caused me. If he did, I doubt he would care. Mr Angry's influence on the world is negative and, although actions tend to be exaggerated when people get behind the wheel, I would hazard a guess that the Mr and Mrs Angrys of this world cause a whole heap of negativity to be sent out into the universe and probably aren't really bothered about that fact at all.

I don't want to be one of them.

If I'm honest with myself, even at my worst I rarely act like a raging road hog. I'm rarely angry or aggressive. What I can quite often be, which is every bit as destructive, is what my friend Bev refers to as a 'mood hoover'. We all know them, people who seem to suck the joy and goodness out of every situation. Folks who have a negative retort for every suggestion we make. Who drag us down. Who drag everybody down. The people you don't want to invite to the figurative party of life because you know they are going to kill the mood stone dead. They remind me of the Dementors in the Harry Potter stories. I fear, perhaps even know, that I have on many occasions been a mood hoover to my friends and family. Anxiety disorders and depression turn you inward and create a barrier to how everyone else around you is feeling. I have often felt that I am the only person in the world with problems and have been desperately eager to share those problems with others to try and get some relief. I have learned through bitter experience that it doesn't work. All my mood hoovering has ever succeeded in doing is driving people away.

It's not always easy but, as much as I don't want to be around mood hoovers, I also don't want to live with a mood hoover inside my head. I don't want the sum total of my influence on the universe to be negative.

Thankfully, and it may not always seem that way, for every Mr Angry or Mrs Mood Hoover there are at least ten Starfish Throwers.

Yes, you've probably heard the story of the starfish thrower. A man was walking along a beach one day and he noticed a boy throwing starfish into the sea.

'What are you doing?' asked the man.

'Throwing the starfish back into the sea,' said the boy. 'They've been stranded on the beach and if I don't throw them back they will die.'

The man looked at the boy incredulously. He then looked at the massive expanse of beach and the thousands of starfish littered across the shore.

'That's ridiculous,' scorned the man. 'You'll never throw them all back before they die, you can't possibly make a difference!'

'True,' said the boy, looking at the starfish in his hand, 'but I can make a difference to this one,' and he hurled the creature back into the sea and turned around to continue his work.

Starfish throwers know they can't make a difference to everyone but, if the opportunity arises, they will make a difference to *someone*. A smile; a listening ear; a helping hand; a random act of kindness; just being there in someone else's Slough of Despond. Being brave enough to offer help and risk rejection, to let compassion outweigh fear. Starfish throwers deserve medals but rarely even get thanks. That doesn't mean that their efforts are in vain. The impact their butterfly wings can have on the ripples of this chaotic life are often immeasurable.

In my life I have been so grateful for starfish throwers. I can honestly say that the kindness of strangers has given me that little bit of strength I have needed to continue through the day on many an occasion. Take the two ordinary angels I mentioned in the prologue who helped me at the checkout. I never knew their names, wouldn't know them again if I sat next to them on a bus, but they were there when I needed them. They didn't treat me as a crazy woman, they reached out ever so slightly to show me that I wasn't alone. Then there was the woman who tried to help when I was freaking out in my car outside IKEA. She may have felt impotent and I may have shooed her away, too embarrassed to draw her into my drama, but she calmed me and focused me on the present just long enough for me to call my friends for help. There are many more people who have touched my life in small but similar ways. Too many to remember let alone mention. We brush past people on our journey and whether we leave behind the aroma of kindness or the stink of animosity is largely up to us.

Never underestimate the effort it takes some people to get from one end of the day to the other. Never underestimate the effect a small random act of kindness can have on another person's journey. I hope that when the final reckoning is done I will have done more starfish throwing than mood hoovering. I hope that, if only once, I could be a positive part of someone else's story.

'Your battles inspired me – not the obvious material battles but those that were fought and won behind your forehead.'

James Joyce

While mental illness, grief, loneliness or life's worries might give us a propensity towards the negative it doesn't have to be that way. While it might make starfish throwing a more colossal task it doesn't make it impossible. People with mental illness may often be perceived by the world as weak, but some of the greatest thinkers and artists that have ever existed have been plagued with depression, anxieties and psychosis. Take Vincent Van Gogh: a prolific painter he failed to sell any but one of the 900 paintings he produced in his lifetime. He was hospitalised several times with periods of mental illness and eventually took his own life at the age of thirty-seven. Since then his artwork has brought joy to generations. His paintings sell for hundreds of millions of dollars. He was an artistic genius whose influence reached around the world. Unfortunately he never lived to see it.

If any work of art accurately captures the angst of mental illness it is *The Scream* by Edvard Munch. Munch toured the edges of insanity for most of his life and because of this was heavily influenced by Van Gogh. The creativity of both of these artists was inspired by their mental turmoil, not stifled by it.

'For as long as I can remember I have suffered from a deep feeling of anxiety which I have tried to express in my art.'

Edvard Munch

One of my favourite movies is the beautiful Oscar-winning film *Shine*, which portrays the biography of David Helfgott, the internationally renowned concert pianist. Helfgott developed mental illness while studying at the Royal School of Music in London in the seventies and subsequently spent many years in psychiatric institutions. It may have seemed for many years that Helfgott's career was over and any hope of a fulfilling life had been long since forgotten. However, today David has been married to a woman who adores him for over thirty years and has had a long and successful musical career. He tours every year and his ability to manipulate a piano keyboard is astounding. I could watch the film *Shine* again and again and again. I've never seen Helfgott play in person (although there are a multitude of videos of him on YouTube), but Geoffrey Rush's performance has me crying, then laughing, then crying with laughter every time. I never cease to watch the film without feeling inspired. True, I don't have Helfgott's extraordinary talent, but then neither has my demise into mental ill health been as extreme or unforgiving as his. If he can return from the brink of insanity and lead a rewarding life, so can I.

How many more people can I name who have had an influence on me? John Nash, the *A Beautiful Mind* mathematician, who was considered a genius in his field despite his schizophrenia. Winston Churchill who was plagued by his black dog of depression; Charles Darwin suffered from a panic disorder, Beethoven was bipolar, Donny Osmond has social phobia, Robin Williams made millions of people laugh but he was plagued by depression and self-doubt. I could go on and on and on. The list is endless. Frequently genius and mental ill health go hand in hand. Is that because they are so closely linked or just because mental illness is so common that it is a statistical certainty that it will affect a good proportion of geniuses and high achievers?

Tips from my Toolbox: Hobbies and creativity

Lord Byron once said, 'If I don't write to empty my mind I go mad.' Byron lived in the quieter times of the nineteenth century before information overload bombarded us with tweets, websites, 24/7 TV, and instant access to our workplace and social lives though mobile phones and Wi-Fi networks. Even in the gentile and relatively slow-paced era of the early 1800s Byron's head became so crowded with thoughts that the need to express those thoughts in writing became a compulsion rather than a casual whim.

'If I don't write to empty my mind, I go mad.'

Lord Byron

My head gets crowded, often with negative thoughts, frequently with worries, sometimes just with information. Recently my smartphone (which is not so much smart as downright cocky) has decided to start announcing the latest news headlines with a loud sound bite of the BBC news theme tune. I didn't ask it to do this, I didn't alter any settings. I have no idea how to switch it off. As well as being bombarded by tweets, status updates, emails and texts I now know instantly all the latest news happening worldwide. It doesn't help that I carry my phone around like a talisman, anxious when it rings, worried when it doesn't. Scouring Facebook at every opportunity, feeling drained when I get another follower on Twitter, becoming discouraged if my post doesn't get the requisite number of 'likes'. My name is Gail Mitchell and I am a social media addict. I need to go cold turkey but I fear the world might end if I do!

So what does all this have to do with Lord Byron and hobbies?

At the moment writing for me is a hobby. Albeit a therapeutic hobby which I hope one day will be lucrative it is, at present, no more than a pastime, but what a way to pass time!

From the earliest age at which I learned to put pen to paper I have used writing as a way to still my tumultuous mind and focus my ideas on something outside myself. When writing I can forget the 637 worries and insecurities which are tumbling around my brain at every given moment. Whether I am creating an alternate reality in the form of a short story or expressing my opinions in a blog or writing a poem to pour out my inner angst, I am totally focused on the keyboard or notepad. I have to concentrate all my attention not just on content but also on syntax, spelling and grammar. It absorbs me so fully that I don't have time to worry or feel depressed.

I would never dare to compare myself with Van Gogh or Byron or David Helfgott but I do find that there is link between creativity and mental illness. Some of my best poetry has come when I'm depressed, some of my primary inspiration has come when I have locked myself away from the world.

I used to think I didn't have time for hobbies and felt guilty for spending time on myself and by myself. Now I realise it is so important to my wellbeing that I must make time, especially when I am busy, because that is the time when I am most likely to fall prey to an anxiety overload. I frequently add 'writing' (or 'calligraphy' or 'learn Portuguese') to my daily To Do list. These things are as essential to me as eating and getting dressed, much more important than responding to emails or reconciling the bank statement.

Hobbies are things I do for myself by myself, which may seem selfish but someone once gave me a very useful analogy which has stuck with me ever since. When you watch the safety announcement by the flight attendants before taking off in an aeroplane, they always, without fail, tell you to put your own oxygen mask on before helping others to put on theirs. Let me say that again. Put your own oxygen mask on before helping others to put on theirs. Even your own children who you love more than life itself. If you're not getting oxygen to your own brain you are no use to anyone else. It may go against every well-mannered notion you have ever been taught, but you are no good to anyone else unless you look after yourself first.

Put your own oxygen mask on before helping others to put on theirs.

Flight safety announcement

As for having time? There are 168 hours in a week. I sleep for seventy of those hours and work for forty. That leaves fifty-eight hours unaccounted for. Fifty-eight hours! That's mammoth! Even if I deduct time for housework, voluntary work, family and social commitments there is no excuse for me not to find at least thirty minutes a day to absorb myself in a nourishing activity. After all, I find time to watch soaps, surf the internet, trawl social media and fret about the state of the world in general. Can I really not spare half an hour for something which will enrich and heal my life?

Over to You: Hobbies and creativity

- Decide which hobbies or pastimes give you a positive sense of wellbeing. The list is as endless as the number of people who need to find ways to pass their leisure time. You will know when you have found it though, because it will give you a mini holiday from the worrying realities of life. Some examples might include:

  - Crafts
  - Cryptic crosswords
  - Reading novels
  - Jigsaws
  - Cinema
  - Walking
  - Learning Portuguese
  - Gardening
  - Painting
  - Playing a musical instrument
  - Team sports
  - Running
  - Baking

- Consider if you are the sort of person who benefits from solitary hobbies or pastimes performed as a group or maybe a balance of both.

- Think you don't have time to indulge yourself? There are 168 hours in week: where can you fit in a couple of hours during that week for yourself? If every one of those 168 hours is taken up with the demands of other people then you, more than any of us, need to eke out some time for yourself.

Enjoying yourself helps beat stress. Doing an activity you enjoy probably means you're good at it and achieving something boosts your self-esteem.

Concentrating on a hobby like gardening or the crossword can help you forget your worries for a while and change your mood.

www.mentalhealth.org.uk, reproduced with kind permission

I'm not alone in giving this advice. Many practitioners including the Mental Health Foundation recommend losing yourself in a hobby to distract you from your worries. For me it is important to discipline myself to do this when I am well to keep me well. It is much harder to pick up your paintbrush, gardening trowel or guitar when you are low, but developing a hobby habit will not only help maintain a positive state of mind: if it becomes part of your routine, it will be easier to pick up on 'auto-pilot' on the days when even getting out of bed is a trial of Herculean proportions.

When I'm writing (or reading a good book or tackling a cryptic crossword) I forget to check my Twitter feed or obsess because my text hasn't been replied to. I'm too busy to fret, I overlook my constant need to worry. I get an endorphin rush from having created or achieved something (even if it's only to have an epiphany about the double meaning of 11 across).

I hope you too will find some glorious relief in an absorbing hobby. Maybe you will create a work of art that will hang in the Tate, or write a bestseller, or start a cottage industry? Or maybe you will just find an hour or two of bliss in the corner of a busy and stressful week. Enjoy!

* * *

All the people mentioned above and more have affected my life in a positive way, but there is one more story I must recount of a small yet magnificent act which has influenced me to try and become a better person and always do the right thing.

I know nothing about mountain climbing, except that it is very difficult and completely beyond my physical ability; I puff and pant up one flight of stairs. I have a passing respect for people who have climbed Mount Everest but apart from Edmund Hillary and Tenzing Norgay I would have had no idea how many other people had ever attempted the feat let alone be able to name them. That is until Martyn Joseph wrote a song called 'Walk Down the Mountain' and introduced the story behind it while I was sat in the audience of one of his concerts at Derby Assembly Rooms. The song is about Dr Beck Weathers. If Beck Weathers wanted to be famous for anything it was as someone who reached the summit of the highest peak in the world. As it happens he achieved notoriety for something much more amazing and, in fact, it was precisely because he failed to reach his goal.

Beck Weathers was an obsessive climber who battled with suicidal depression. Whether the two went hand in hand probably only he knows. In 1996 Beck left his comfortable home and family in the USA to attempt to climb Everest. His wife was ready to end their marriage because of Beck's climbing obsession. This didn't deter him. Unfortunately he chose one of the worst times in the history of the mountain to attempt the ascent. A devastating storm hit, taking experienced climbers and novices by surprise. For various reasons, which you can read about in his book, *Left For Dead*, Beck got separated from most of his group as they were trying to return down the mountain to the relative safety of their camp. Beck suffered severe frostbite and fell into a hypothermic coma. When rescuers found his body on the mountain they realised he was as good as dead, no one had ever come out of a hypothermic coma on a mountainside, and they left his body where it lay.

By some miracle that we may never understand, Beck woke up and then, by some super-human effort of will, he stood up and stumbled half blind, half crazed, and somehow found his way back to the rest of his group. The rest of them that is who hadn't died on the mountainside.

Even then his prognosis was poor. He had frostbite on both hands, his face was black and his vital signs were weakening. This was not base camp, just a group of tents with minimal medical supplies and a huge emergency to deal with. They put Beck in a tent, made him comfortable and left him to die during the night.

He didn't die. He recovered, went home, rebuilt his marriage and his life with two amputated hands and a face reconstructed by plastic surgery.

Beck Weathers' story inspired me. Not that he put his marriage at risk to climb a mountain; that doesn't impress me at all. I'm maybe a little inspired by the fact there was some miracle that woke him up on that mountain and that he found quite a bit inside (or outside?) himself that gave him the strength of will to walk down the mountain. True, I am in awe of him for rebuilding his life after such a traumatic experience and devastating injuries and it gives me some kind of warm feeling that he admits that his mountaintop experience cured him of his depression and helped him to see the joy in every day.

Yet none of those things are what gave me goosebumps as Martyn recounted Beck's adventures over a decade later in a small auditorium in the middle of England. No, why Beck Weathers will forever be on my list of heroes is this…

Once Beck had reached Camp Two there was no way he could get further down the mountain. Both his hands were useless and his only option was an airlift, but that was no option at all. No helicopter had ever flown that high, the lack of air pressure wouldn't allow the copter to stay in the air. It couldn't be done. Despite cheating death on not one but two occasions, it looked like Beck was finally beaten.

Beck's wife did not know it couldn't be done. From her home in Texas she called in every favour she could think of, she rang politicians, professors, journalists until her pleas reached Lt. Col. Madan K C, a Nepalese pilot who was willing to risk his own life to save Beck's. That pilot was a hero in a day of heroes. He took the flight without a co-pilot (to minimise the weight) and with as little equipment as he could get away with. He knew it couldn't be done but he was willing to try to save the life of an American he had never met.

Even that is not the bit that gives me shivers every time I think about it.

At the same time as Beck was lying dying on the mountain waiting for the helicopter that had no chance of arriving and which his wife had moved heaven and earth to get, another injured climber was brought into camp. Makalu Gau also had no chance of getting down the mountain under his own steam. He too needed an airlift for any chance of life. The helicopter, if it made it at all, could only take one person. It had Beck's name on it but when it miraculously arrived at the camp Beck let Makalu Gau take the only ride out of there. Never mind that he himself was dying, that he had used every ounce of physical strength and mettle to get him this far; never mind that the helicopter had come especially for him and no one else, he gave his chance of escape up for a stranger.

That is what makes me go goosepimply all over.

He knew without that ride he would die. He was at the weakest, lowest point he had ever been in his life, he had every right to that helicopter ride, but he gave it up for a stranger. He said it 'seemed like the right thing to do.'

That is why Beck Weathers is my hero. Because when push came to shove, when the chips were down, when all platitudes were said and done, when he was staring death in the face and when nobody was looking – he did the right thing.

'When we were up there, we didn't think anybody was looking and so everybody did pretty much what their inner person, the real them, the exposed them, would do. And some individuals come out of that, I think, justly proud of their actions. Others would probably never want anybody to know.'

Beck Weathers

Anyone can do the right thing when it's easy and there's time to think and the cost is not great, but I want to be like Beck Weathers. If I'm ever remembered for anything in this world, I want it to be that, at the worst possible moment when I was weak and afraid and alone, I did the right thing. I'm the first to admit that hasn't always been the case so far in my life. I can't do anything about that, but if my darkest hour is still to come I hope I will remember Beck and his helicopter and I will do the right thing, even if no one is looking and no one will ever know.

CHAPTER TEN

The Tiny Mustard Seed of Faith

I'm lucky enough never to have needed the support of a group such as Alcoholics Anonymous. I've never truly been addicted to anything. Although I often crave chips, coffee and sleep I can see how easy it would be to become hooked on tobacco, drugs or gambling. From what I've learned of the methods of 'Anonymous' groups over the years, I can appreciate why they have such a high success rate and are so well respected in the field of addiction intervention. From what I can gather their method relies on two key elements: first, the support of another addict, a sponsor, who is further along the road to recovery than the individual, and second, the renowned twelve-step programme.

The support of someone who has travelled a similar journey to us is something we can all use from time to time. It is essentially what I am aiming to do with this book, to share some of my experiences with you so you can, in turn, share some of your experiences with others. The twelve-step programme is maybe something we are less familiar with, but a key component of it is having faith in a higher being than ourselves. It doesn't prescribe a God of any particular faith or creed but recognises the need for prayer, meditation and an improved contact with God, however we perceive Him. Steps two and three of the twelve-step programme (as taken from the AA of Great Britain website) are as follows:

1. We came to believe that a Power greater than ourselves could restore us to sanity.
2. We made a decision to turn our will and our lives over to the care of God as we understood Him.

I've never followed the twelve steps but no description of the many fluctuations of my mental state would be complete without acknowledging the part faith has played in it. I say faith and not religion because there has always been a battle within me between the two. I believe that any analysis of ourselves, any deep soul-searching, can only ever be productive by recognising the spiritual as well as the cerebral.

'We are not human beings having a spiritual experience. We are spiritual beings having a human experience.'

Pierre Teilhard de Chardin

People often say things like 'Oh at least she has her faith – it must be a comfort for her,' or worse they describe faith as something of a crutch for the weak which stronger people can do without. Faith isn't a nice cuddly teddy bear – it isn't a security blanket. It's a challenging way of being. Yes there is comfort and strength in having faith in a higher being, yes I believe prayer and meditation can help through life's trials, and I also believe that prayer can alter the circumstances we experience, but as for easy? No way, Jose!

I can only really talk about my experiences within a Christian setting and my perception of a Christian God, but I do believe there is only one God and I have respect for all spiritual seekers however they experience that one omnipresence. Following a faith, trying to love and share when hate and dominance are the natural predications, trying to avoid temptation, trying to hope when all you feel in your heart is despair and failure, this is not easy. As G K Chesterton so eloquently put it: 'Christianity has not been tried and found wanting; it has been found difficult and not tried!'

> Research literature has consistently reported that aspects of religious and spiritual involvement are associated with desirable mental health outcomes.
>
> The Royal College of Psychiatrists notes that people who use mental health services identify the benefits of good quality spiritual care as being: improved self-control, self-esteem and confidence; speedier and easier recovery; and improved relationships.
>
> *Fundamental Facts About Mental Health*,
> Mental Health Foundation, reproduced with kind permission

Faith and the Life Less Lived are as intertwined as steak and kidney, Ant and Dec, laughter and tears. Faith looks at the spiritual as preferential to the material. The Life Less Lived appreciates weakness and winding paths; the spiritual path is narrow and circuitous and rocky. It's a climb to a destination that we can never quite see, will never quite reach in this life. Often its roads are hidden and mysterious. Believe me, if you are living, and loving, the Life Less Lived, you are further along your spiritual journey than you may think.

Tips from my Toolbox: Mindfulness

Every morning I commute to work, either by car or on the Nottingham City tram network. When I travel by tram it seems that every single passenger, including myself, is plugged in. If they don't have earphones wired for sound they are reading a

Kindle reader or scrolling up and down their three-inch mobile screens trying to connect with the world while completely oblivious to what is actually going on around them.

True, a daily commute is boring. It is a tedious waste of time. Yet this particular morning I decided to use it to practise my mindfulness rather than catch up on the latest YouTube videos. I sat in my seat and took long deep breaths and tried to become attuned to my environment. I let thoughts slip through my head without dwelling on them. I focused on the sights and sounds presented to me through my journey. I tried to picture myself as a young child, experiencing all this for the first time. I aimed for a curious and open attitude.

Not only was it way more relaxing than scrunching up my eyes staring at Facebook while the trams shunting and bumping triggered slight travel-sick nausea, it was an astonishing, verging on spiritual, experience. I saw things I'd never seen before, even though I'd travelled this journey hundreds of times. Yes, some of these insights were trivial, like the fact that Nottingham Express Transit waste bins have a trendy, ergonomic design and that Hyson Green Market is open on Wednesdays and Saturdays. However, I also saw the most amazing sky, spattered with oranges, pinks and purples against a backdrop of the palest blue imaginable. It cast a beautiful canopy over the whole of Nottingham as though Jackson Pollock and Banksy had had an amazingly talented love child (if that were biologically possible – which it may be – who says Banksy is a man?) who had painted a stunning gift to the people of the city. People who, if they are anything like I usually am on a weekday morning, would never have looked away from social media long enough to appreciate it.

Mindfulness is one of the buzzwords of our age. You don't have to look very far to find books, podcasts, articles or classes about mindfulness. Unlike some of the other weird crazes pervading our society, mindfulness has good reason to be popular.

I first experienced it when I was fortunate enough to have been referred to a mindfulness group by the NHS. It was for people recovering from anxiety and depression and the aim of the eight-week class was to avoid relapses in our condition. This was a few years ago and I can't say it completely prevented any further downward spirals, but then again I can't say I practised it religiously every day either.

What I can say with certainty is that mindfulness has helped me stay on an even keel and, even though I probably only do it for a maximum of three minutes a day, it has helped me stay focused on what is real and what is simply a figment of my over-active, anxious imagination.

> *You only have to let the soft animal of your body*
> *love what it loves.*
> *Tell me about despair, yours, and I will tell you mine.*
> *Meanwhile the world goes on...*
>
> Extract from *'Wild Geese'* by Mary Oliver

Many of us don't experience what is around us. We travel through life on autopilot, our mind full of what might happen, what should happen, what did or didn't happen, instead of focusing on the present moment and what is actually happening. If you are a driver, have you ever driven somewhere and then had no recollection of how you got there? Or even worse, set out to go somewhere but automatically headed somewhere else? We are not present in the moment – and that can lead to anxiety and depression, or at the very least a wasted experience.

Ironically, fitting the mindfulness classes into my life became very stressful and self-defeating at first. I had to travel nearly an hour to the classes and often arrived stressed and flustered, which was exacerbated by the fact that I attended the group at the end of a busy working day. We did mindfulness exercises in class but I wasn't very good at them and felt inadequate compared to the others who seemed to get much more out of it than me. Moreover, we had to make a commitment to practise our mindfulness exercises for forty minutes a day. I found this impossible to fit in and, at the end of the day when I tried, I invariably fell asleep within the first few minutes and would wake up a couple of hours later when the CD had finished its cycle, not having been mindful about anything at all!

Gradually it dawned on me that I was missing the point. The first rule of mindfulness is to let go of any expectations about what it will do for you. You're not aiming to feel relaxed, you're just aiming to experience whatever it is you are feeling in that moment and examine it with kindness and gentle interest. Or, as it said in the manual that accompanied the course, the easiest way to relax is to stop trying to make things different.

I can't, in one chapter, give you a full introduction to mindfulness. What I can tell you is what I have learned from the short course and subsequent practice of this wonderful art.

When you drink, just drink
When you walk, just walk

Zen saying

I have learned to let go of ideas of success and failure, to stop labelling my experiences and to approach each new encounter with gentle curiosity. It's so easy to think things like, 'I'm having a stressful day,' 'This is going to be really bad,' 'I handled that situation like an idiot.' Labelling experiences leads to negative thoughts, which lead to anxious and depressing feelings. Instead, wherever possible, I just try and go with the flow and have a curious attitude to what is happening.

A common one for me is to make a mistake at work. My auto-response is 'I'm going to get into trouble, the boss will be angry, I'll have a panic attack, I'll end up leaving my job and be back on benefits, I am a failure.' It can take a split second to pass through all these thoughts and before I know it I am actually experiencing the feelings of self-loathing, disgust and panic that come with leaving a job through anxiety. Nothing has actually happened but I feel as though it has.

Now I am slowly learning to take a step away from such spiralling thoughts and step back into the present moment. At this moment I am safe. At this moment I am well. At this moment nothing bad is happening. I will approach telling my boss with gentle curiosity. At this moment I am not a failure, I am just human. The sun is still shining, I am still loved, the world is an OK place to be.

From mindfulness I have also learned how automatic and subconscious our thoughts can be. On the course I attended they likened it to getting on The Worry Train. In the example above there is a distinct point where I mounted The Worry Train; however, often I don't know where or when I got on and I can be halfway to Destination Disaster before I even realise what my mind is up to. With mindfulness I am able to stop, track back my thoughts, and see where these panicky, mixed-up emotions came from. When I do so I usually find it is something so trivial that it's hard to believe I got so worked up so automatically.

Mindfulness also teaches you to let thoughts flow through your mind rather than dwell on them. How often do we replay the same situation over and over in our minds, and in doing so replay the emotions in our bodies? With mindfulness you don't fight such thoughts, you just look at them with kindness and inquisitiveness and let them pass by. You don't judge yourself if the thoughts come back – after all, that is the natural way of the human brain – you just look at them again and send them on their way. Some people find it helps to imagine themselves looking at their thoughts playing out on a cinema screen. I find it helps to see them as clouds floating by.

Another important part of mindfulness is not to judge our thoughts, and not to judge ourselves for having those thoughts. Thoughts come and go. Some are good, some are bad. If we get frustrated at our negative thoughts we give fuel to them, and to the emotions they evoke. Just examine them, wonder at them and then let them pass by. Anyway, thoughts are not facts. They may be very real to us, but they are just figments of our imagination. We are not fortune tellers. We have no knowledge of what will happen in the next moment to this, or the next, or any time in the future. We are not mind readers. We do not know that that person thought we were stupid, or didn't like us, or is obsessing about us in the same way we are obsessing about them. More than likely they have gone on their way, caught up in their own worries and woes, not giving us a second thought.

In Nottinghamshire there is a charity called Each Amazing Breath. It aims to 'enhance wellbeing, self-care and control and personal performance.' As far as I know it has nothing to do with mindfulness but its name captured my imagination partly because of my experience with the practice. One of the first exercises we learned in class was to connect with our breath. Every second of our lives we breathe in and breathe out. It is an essential lifeline that we rarely consider or give a moment's thought to. Focusing on the ins and outs of our lungs, concentrating on the sensations in our mouth, nose and stomach, is a simple technique to bring us back to the here and now. Each breath we take is an amazing miracle of nature and focusing on its gentle rhythms is a perfect starting point for taking us out of our imagination and in touch with our physical presence.

Mindfulness can be a very spiritual experience, although it is very different to prayer and even to meditation; it does, however, bring a sense of what really matters and what is just peripheral noise. There is nothing religious about mindfulness (I don't think they'd allow it on the NHS if there was?), but I personally find that, through mindfulness, I can come to a new understanding of my circumstances and myself. If prayer is talking to an external being, mindfulness is stopping talking and just listening, just experiencing, just being.

Over to You: Mindfulness

Mindfulness takes practice and there is a lot more to it than I have covered here, so I would advise borrowing a book or finding a local class or maybe asking your GP. In the meantime, right now you can try these quick tips:

- 'When you drink, just drink. When you walk, just walk' (Zen saying).
- Let go of expectations and labels, of ideas of success and failure, of pain and comfort. Just notice what is within and without you with a sense of curiosity.
- Look out for when your mind goes on the Worry Train, which it will do many times a day, and each time gently and kindly bring your attention back to the present.
- Never berate yourself for how many times you need to bring your mind back to the present. Mindfulness isn't about being calm or comfortable; it is about noticing and experiencing things as they are now.
- As often as you can throughout the day take short breaks to notice and concentrate on each amazing breath.
- Short bursts can be more manageable than long meditation sessions because it is very easy to fit several five-minute mindfulness 'holidays' into your day: on the commute to work, while eating your dinner, doing a hobby, taking a walk.

* * *

My spiritual journey is not a great inspiration to anyone. I have 'up'ed, 'down'ed, 'in'ed and 'out'ed more times than I care to remember and I have spent more than my fair share of time in the Slough of Despond, but I have held on. As a Christian I am an abject failure, my faith is so small that it is hardly noticeable to those around me, but I have never completely given up.

I have at times been part of churches; I now only attend occasionally. I find 'church' very difficult. I have social phobia, I can't relax in big crowds. That's only one of the many reasons. I find churches confusing, demanding, hard work. They drain me. I find God in silence and solitude. I find him on hillsides and beside lakes. I find him in my bible and in secular works of fiction, in the people I meet on the tram, at home and at work. Apart from that, I question too much for people to feel comfortable around me, I doubt when certainty is the order of the day, I don't really 'get' all the traditions or rules. I try and focus on the fact that Jesus said, Love God, love your neighbour, love yourself, that's it (and I apologise for paraphrasing his great words, which can be found in Chapter 10 of Luke's gospel, verse 27).

I decided long ago that all my spiritual and religious efforts would be concentrated on those three commandments. If I could get them off pat then I'd worry about which denomination was best or whether to sing hymns or choruses or just sit in silence.

I have totally failed to love God, or my neighbour or myself for even one day!

I'm totally rubbish at it! But it does give me something to work with, some kind of moral compass to measure all my aspirations against. I may fall woefully short of target but I keep on shooting for the goal.

Notice the bit about loving yourself? The actual words are 'love your neighbour in the same way as you love yourself.' I found this particularly challenging especially with all my mental anxieties. How could I love people if I didn't love myself? I didn't even like myself?

This is a huge lesson that I have had to learn, which didn't come in any kind of revelation so much as a growing realisation. How can you treat other people right if you don't treat yourself right? If you continually beat yourself with a big stick how can you stop criticising and blaming the world around you?

The other thing I realised is that love is a doing word much more than it is a feeling word. Taking care of myself and my needs even when I didn't feel like it is part of loving myself (in the same way a parent will love and care for their offspring even if they are really mad at them). The more I took care of myself, the better I felt about myself and the more time I had for the people around me who needed me to care for them, too.

Don't get me wrong, I'm no guru. I get it wrong ALL the time! Maybe in ten years I'll write another book exactly on this topic but at present I am very much the novice.

Someone who certainly wasn't a novice in spiritual matters was the principal of the college that I attended in Bristol. He was old school. He was phenomenally clever and I often wonder what he made of ignorant and rebellious me. I like to think I challenged his thinking, but that is unlikely. I think he'd seen people like me before and he has seen people come along after. I think he was unfazed by my presence.

So what was it about this wise old man which has stuck with me over the years? Often I have tried to be someone I'm not: a calm person; a person without mental health issues; a good Christian; a team player; one of the gang; a successful business woman. The Rev. Dr Brian Haymes once told me that when I get to the pearly gates God isn't going to say to me, 'Why weren't you Rosa Parks?', 'Why weren't you J K Rowling?', 'Why weren't you Steve Jobs?' He will say to me, 'Why weren't you Gail Mitchell?'

Why wasn't I Gail Mitchell?

As we go through the daily jumps and hurdles of this thing we call life we don't have to be anything more or less than ourselves. As Angela Leaney said in the talk that inspired me to take up my pen and write this book (see page xiii), we each have our unique skill set. We each have our own strengths and gifts to offer. No one (no one who matters anyway) either in this material or any other spiritual realm is asking us to be anything more than who we are.

What a huge relief that is!

What a weight of anxiety and self-loathing lifts from my chest. I may panic, I may be a solitary loner, I may hate singing hymns, but get this. That's the way I was made! It's the way I was destined to be!

Aside from the fact it can often take a lifetime to work out who we really are! Like I said I don't have all the answers; being honest with yourself and about yourself isn't easy... I'm waiting for the sequel, when I have all the answers and can write eloquently a 'How to Find Yourself and Believe in Yourself Guide'! Available from all good book stores, in about fifteen years, when I might have figured out some of the answers!

Do not expect to find all the answers of this world
'cos if we could somehow and then we did, well
Who would we be?

But if you're drifting away
If it's falling apart

Just let yourself,
Be quietly drawn by the stronger call of what you really love
Let your soul,
The one that you brought with you safe
to this moment in time

Whisper to your fears
And wrestle with the noise of this night,
for you
And in the midst of these moments
It's like we never left
But in a lifetime of returning
We're not home yet, we're not home yet

Extract from 'Let Yourself' by Martyn Joseph
Reproduced with kind permission

Someone who has helped me a long way on the journey of self-discovery is Sister Monica. For four or five years I visited Sister Monica every three months at the local convent in Derbyshire where she was then Mother Superior. It was suggested to me that I seek Monica out for spiritual direction. This was an Anglican sisterhood but I'm neither Catholic nor Anglican and I knew next to nothing about nuns and their calling. I was trepidatious, to say the least. I was struggling with the guilt of not attending church while at the same time panicking and running away every time I tried to venture to be part of any sort of community. What could a woman who had deliberately chosen a vow of poverty and chosen to spend all her days and nights in the company of sisters from another mother have to say to me? How could she even begin to understand?

Over those five years we sat at intervals in her first-floor study, which overlooked the trees and tranquil grounds of the convent, and I poured my turbulent musings out to Monica. They made no sense to me as they tumbled out of my brain, but somehow in her wisdom and sensitivity she looked at all my entrails of anxiety and gave them back to me in a beautiful gift wrap that made me believe that rather than an abject failure I was a talented, valued and gifted individual. Monica took each of my failures and showed me the strength hidden within. Oh that everyone could have a Sister Monica to walk beside! The world would be a much better place.

Without food man can survive for barely thirty days; without water for little more than three days; without air hardly for more than three minutes; but without hope he might destroy himself in even shorter time.

From *The Conduct of Life* by Lewis Mumford

With her I could be honest and open about death, depression, despair and guilt. Monica is one of the few who never tried to mould or nurture me into something I'm not. Instead she encouraged me to be the person I was created to be. In that, she reflected more of God to me than any amount of sermonising or church activity.

Monica encouraged my writing, she encouraged my relationship with my partner, she encouraged my solitude. She accepted me! She made me aware that God is bigger than any idea of him that we can create. He is more than all the preconceptions we have of him. Monica laid down not one single rule about how I should live or who I should be, and in that acceptance gave me an understanding of faith that was more spiritual and holy than anything I have experienced.

So my faith is often as small as the proverbial mustard seed, but it is still part of my DNA. Despite all my cynicism and criticism I have also had some truly awesome moments in my life where the veil between heaven and earth has been so thin as to be transparent. To go back to the wording of the AA steps one and two I have come (hesitantly) to believe that a Power greater than ourselves could restore us to sanity and I have made a decision (albeit one which I have reneged on many times) to turn my will and my life over to the care of God as I understand Him.

In the Greek legend that you are probably familiar with, Pandora's curiosity led her to open her jar and let out all the evil and wickedness into the world. Pandora tried to recapture and contain everything in the box but couldn't. All she could catch was hope. The legend is meant to give an explanation of all of the world's woes; however, for me the key point has always been the final one. At the end of the story Pandora still had hope. Without hope we are… well, utterly depressed for one thing.

So for all my doubts I will cling on to my little mustard seed. This Power greater than myself who I choose to call God has been there when I was too desperate to even consider his presence; he has led me along the Life Less Lived when I didn't even know I needed a guide. In the words of Psalm 84 I'd rather be a door-keeper in the house of the Lord and only stay a day, than live the life of a sinner and have to stay away. Or, as I wrote in one particularly dark and desperate time when I was utterly depressed and hopeless:

> *I must believe that, deep within,*
> *There lives some ounce of good something to love in me*
> *Which, on the other side of time,*
> *Will from this bondaged cage be free.*
> *I must believe that travels in this foreign land*
> *Where all are strange and different*
> *Will but pass, as shadows on a moonlit wall.*
> *That when I'm home, these days and years*
> *Will fade and dim*
> *If they are remembered there at all.*

Gail Mitchell

CHAPTER ELEVEN

What If? And Why Not?

I often wonder how my life would have turned out if I hadn't lived with mental illness all these years, if I hadn't discovered the Life Less Lived and learned to love it? What would my life be like and, more importantly, what would *I* be like?

Supposing I could hop into some parallel universe, the one where I'd been 'sane' and 'normal' and just carried on my projected path from my O levels to now? Then suppose I could meet up with the other me and sit and have a drink with her: what would we make of each other?

Well, first of all, I'd be in some quiet coffee shop in the middle of the afternoon and she'd be in some loud and trendy wine bar drinking G&T to unwind after finishing work at about 10 p.m., so the chances of us ever meeting up would be slim. If I did see her, I'd probably give her a wide berth because she would be loud and bossy and too full of her own self-importance and she certainly wouldn't have had time for me, probably having pegged me as some woosy liberal loser at first glance.

This other me would be successful, hardworking, driven and incredibly boring! I'd like to think she would have left accountancy to become CEO of some profitable business venture, which would then have gone from strength to strength. My ambition was always to be chairperson of ICI – not because I had any interest in the workings of ICI but because the job always seemed a sensible combination of my chemical and accounting knowledge. It wouldn't have occurred to me to do a job I enjoyed! It would have been all about how far up the greasy pole I could climb, how quickly I could burst through the glass ceiling; it would have given me a sense of achievement, but really it would have been all about how I appeared to the world.

I wonder if I would have had any sort of life outside of work. I know that I would have got up early every morning eager to head to the office. I would probably have been slightly more reluctant to stay late but it would have been about appearances and I would know (in my head if not in reality) that a CEO shouldn't leave the office before 8 p.m. and should be working from home at weekends. I hope I would have had more stamina than I have now! Probably I would have kept myself going with strong black coffee and unwound with alcohol every evening. I would get high on success and how great I thought I was! I would almost certainly have believed the mantra 'work hard, play hard', so would have joined in the squash games and golf tournaments of my colleagues and definitely have frequented hip and expensive bars and restaurants quite oblivious to the fact that I don't like competitive sports or loud clubs and eateries.

I would have travelled and would have enjoyed that. I've always wanted to travel; we had great holidays as children and I've always wanted to see the world, but what would I have really experienced? I would have selected the most exotic and far-flung holidays but would I have ventured far from the swanky hotels and luxury tour buses? I certainly would have given the people in the favelas of São Paulo a wide berth, and in doing so missed their amazing warmth and generosity. I would never have camped in a two-man tent for ten weeks around the States, but I would have missed the life-changing challenges that experience brought with it. I would have seen many tourist spots but I wouldn't have seen the world.

I would have punished myself with draconian diets and forced myself to visit the gym. The same obsessive compulsion that led me to gain A grades in eleven O levels would have driven me to succeed at anything and everything I touched. If I failed at anything (as when I failed my first driving test) I would have flagellated myself repeatedly until I had regrouped, reassessed and retried until I succeeded. Diet, fitness and beauty would have been all about how I looked, not about health or wellbeing.

I often wonder if I would have married. When I was about sixteen (in the real world) I told my nana that I was never getting married and was quite confused when this made her cry.

'But you'll be a spinster,' she sobbed.

'Don't be silly Nana, there's no such thing as spinsters nowadays!' I retorted impatiently.

I must have made it very clear that marriage was never part of my plan because in my early twenties my dad presented me with a lump sum saying, 'This is what I've been saving for your wedding but as you're never getting married I thought you could have it now.'

I was delighted! I think I put it towards buying my first house, which seemed eminently more sensible than spending it on a man!

If I had married it would have been because all my so-called friends were doing it and it seemed like a good lifestyle choice. He would probably have been called Barnaby or Dominic and would be a lawyer or an accountant. Possibly an actuary but definitely something professional and well paid. I would have approached it in the same way I approached a business partnership. I never believed in romantic love... not in either universe... not until I was forty-two at least. Before that I thought it was something that was made up to sell greetings cards, flowers and dating websites!

Certainly my only regret now about my past is that I never had children, but I would have been a terrible mum! I would have expected perfection from any child of mine; failure or weakness would have been an embarrassment. They would have had the best tutors at the best schools and held a permanent sense of bitterness because they could never live up to my exacting expectations.

Maybe the image above is a bit extreme. I'd like to think that some wisdom and sensitivity would have found its way into my personality over the years, but if you had taken the twenty-year-old me and fast-forwarded twenty-five years without passing go, without stopping to have a nervous breakdown, this is exactly what I would have been like. I was hard-hearted and ambitious. I valued material possessions and success. I looked down my nose at people who were poorer or stupider than me. I was not a nice person at all.

'Some people never go crazy. What truly horrible lives they must lead.'

Charles Bukowski

Would it have been so bad? I would have had some money for one thing! And by many standards of society I would 'have it all'. Moreover, what would it feel like not to be afraid of just about everyone and everything all the time? Surely I would swap that?

Mmm maybe, but I wouldn't swap the empathy I have developed over my years of anxiety and depression for all the arrogance and false confidence of my youth. I wouldn't swap the beauty and loveliness of my nearest and dearest with the never-ending search for more material possessions. Wisdom and spiritual depth have no price. Strength of character cannot be bought but must be earned over years. I may have said I was happy in that other world, but I would never have experienced true joy. I know with all my heart that I wouldn't go back and live a different life. I wouldn't swap even one of my mental struggles, not in hindsight at least. I am now where I was always meant to be, even though I never planned this journey.

Tips from my Toolbox: Hypnotherapy

I am a great believer in the power of hypnotherapy to work as a tool to reduce anxiety, phobias, panic attacks and depression. Unfortunately (as is often the case with me), my experiences of it to date have been disastrous and slightly comical.

Recently, I met up with my friend Sally who is a qualified hypnotherapist and runs the Acorn Natural Health Centre in Heanor, Derbyshire. I first met Sally as part of the weight management group I talked about in my tips Eat, Move, Sleep in Chapter 4. I liked Sally because she talked realistically about how the mind works and how to change our thought patterns. Visiting Sally in her practice you get the feeling that you are in safe hands. It is a calm, professional space and Sally gives off an air of proficient efficiency. I trust her knowledge, I trust her common sense; I am a hundred per cent convinced she is not a quack. This week we met up specifically so that I could get Sally's expert opinion on how I can benefit in the future from the healing effects of hypnotherapy and how I can avoid (and help you avoid) a repeat of my earlier disastrous experience with another hypnotherapist!

It was about ten years ago, and I can't remember how I heard about this particular 'hypnotherapist', and I use the word 'hypnotherapist' in the loosest sense of the word. I remember I had his name and number on a scrap of crumpled paper. I hadn't researched him at all, and as far as I'm aware he didn't have a business card or a website. Why warning bells weren't clanging in my brain I will never know; in fact the warning bells didn't start ringing until he turned up on my doorstep in his fancy Jag. He sat down and told me he specialised in weight loss, quitting smoking and other things.

I looked at the man who was getting close to retirement (nothing wrong in that), his massive beer belly, his nicotine-stained fingers, his blood-shot eyes, and took in the smell of tobacco coming off him and thought, 'Seriously?' He was hardly an advert for clean, healthy living. More like a heart attack waiting to happen! Nowadays this is the point I would have kindly asked him to leave and said I had changed my mind. In those days I wasn't assertive enough or I was so desperate that I would give anything a try.

The more he spoke the more I felt like I didn't trust him. I felt creeped out, not relaxed. He told me to lie on my sofa while he spoke/played a tape to me. I was supposed to be getting deeper and deeper into a tranquil state but instead I was on high alert, ready to pounce if he tried to steal the family jewels or… worse!

It didn't help that my only previous contact with a hypnotist was at university when my friend and I went to see a stage hypnotist. My friend volunteered and seemingly acted like a puppet to every whim of the hypnotist puppet master, including ferociously scrubbing the floor and shouting at anyone who walked across it. It was hilarious! But also ever so slightly sinister as she didn't remember a thing about it afterwards, and all I could think lying on my sofa that afternoon was, 'You're not being my puppet master mister!'

Let's be fair, he probably was a genuine guy, but it is no surprise that the hypnotherapy didn't work. I wasn't going to let it! And I paid him for the hour! Oh how I sometimes look at my younger self and say, 'Why oh why? What were you thinking?'

Still, it gave me and Sally something to laugh about when we met up.

I would definitely give hypnotherapy another try. Unfortunately when I first met Sally I was on benefits and not able to afford it, and now I've moved house so it wouldn't be convenient to visit her practice for the sessions. I did quiz her on how to find a good hypnotherapist though, so next time I will be prepared.

'I've gone from masses of anxiety to a person I feel happy with – me! I wish I'd discovered hypnotherapy years ago.'
P K (Testimonial from Acorn Natural Health Centre)

Sally has shared many successes of her work during the time I've known her, but one of the most powerful which sticks in my mind is of a woman who turned up having debilitating panic attacks that appeared to happen quite randomly whenever she saw the colour pink! To such an extent that she would panic if she saw a work colleague in a pink blouse and was unable to enter a shop with a pink window display.

How can the fluffy girly colour pink offend anyone?

As well as wanting to ease these attacks she wanted to know the cause. After several sessions with Sally it turned out that the woman had been in a serious car accident where the car had turned over and over. The woman had thought she was going to die and as the car went round and round all she could see was the pink scarf of another passenger swirling around the car's interior. Afterwards, every time she saw the colour pink her subconscious associated it with the intense, debilitating fear of her near-fatal experience.

Hypnotherapy looks at the automatic associations that our subconscious mind makes and reprogrammes them with more helpful associations. The subconscious mind is like an unruly toddler: it doesn't listen to the reason of the conscious mind and often acts on a kind of autopilot, but in a relaxed dreamlike state it can be retrained. When we try and change a habit or a behavioural pattern we tend to concentrate on what we don't want to happen – I want to stop smoking, I want to stop panicking, I want to stop worrying, which is a bit like not thinking of a pink elephant. As soon as you are told not to think of a pink elephant you immediately think of… the exact thing you are trying to avoid.

Hypnotherapy uses the natural state of mind to help your subconscious focus on what you want – not on what you don't want.

It also helps with the how! You won't spend hours talking about all your problems; instead you will focus on how you want to be.

Over to You: Hypnotherapy

- Choose a reputable therapist: The National Council for Hypnotherapy has a 'Find a Hypnotherapist' section on their website (www.hypnotherapists.org.uk). Anyone on here will be qualified and insured and will undergo rigorous supervision throughout their career.
- Have a free initial consultation with a potential hypnotherapist: if they don't offer this then don't bother with them; even if they are qualified and professional you might not feel comfortable with them and you need to be able to relax with whoever you choose.
- Hypnotherapy can work well for panic attacks, generalised anxiety, phobias, depression, stress and insomnia as well as some physical conditions.
- It's worth asking your GP if hypnotherapy is available on the NHS in your area. It's a bit of a postcode lottery and not one you are likely to win, but it is available in some areas so there is no harm in asking.
- The average cost of a hypnotherapy session is around £60 per hour. This may seem like a lot but not if you think of it as an investment in yourself. It is equivalent to about ten lattes and will do you more good. Not only that, hypnotherapy typically lasts for four to six sessions, a much shorter period than counselling or other forms of therapy.
- For it to work best you need to want to change and be willing to do any 'homework' set between sessions.
- Be assured that no one can make you do anything you don't want to do.

* * *

So what is my life like now? And how is it better than a successful career and a rich husband? Soon after starting this book I
returned to work and I am on a relatively stable mental plain. My
job is perfect for me, second only to being a full-time writer in
the dream job stakes. I work thirty hours a week as an account-
ant/bookkeeper for a local charity. Our clients are other local
charities and not-for-profit organisations, so I meet people from
all walks of life but also spend a lot of time sitting on my own
puzzling over bank reconciliations and sets of accounts, perfect
for a sociophobe like myself. My hours are flexible and my employers and colleagues are human. I have told them about my
anxiety disorder and they take it in their stride; there is something preventative about having understanding and supportive
people around you.

Recently I turned up at the office in tears, so distraught I
couldn't get my words out or make any sense. I was on the verge
of a panic attack. I had a tremendous feeling of déjà vu, another
office, another group of colleagues staring, the foreboding sense
that I would soon be leaving yet another job under a cloud of
mental distress. This time it was different. This time one of my
work mates came up and gave me a hug. Just a brief hug – nothing intrusive (after all, I'm not a touchy-feely person). Then she
made me a cup of tea and we sat down and had a chat. Yes it
took half an hour out of our work day, but within an hour I was
back at my desk working to full efficiency. No thought of going
off sick, no thought of leaving or being dismissed or disciplinary
action. Just me, a slightly imperfect, slightly emotional, slightly
sensitive bookkeeper, with colleagues who accept my weaknesses
as well as my strengths.

I don't have to get everything absolutely right all the time,
although I do feel confident I am pretty good at my job. This is
definitely NOT the sort of job I would have chosen for myself
twenty-five years ago; it doesn't command nearly enough salary

for one thing and certainly doesn't carry a lot of kudos, but it makes a difference to small community groups, is perfect for my lifestyle and state of mind and – I don't care what anyone else thinks – I love it!

After a circuitous and tortuous route through the perils and stresses of teaching and accepting that I don't have what it takes for that particular career, as well as my current day job I still have a small part-time job once a fortnight befriending teenagers. This is long-term work which requires patience and empathy. I have met some amazing girls with heaps of potential but troubled pasts and confused presents in this role. I would like to believe I make a small difference to their futures. They are unlikely to become captains of industry, some have learning difficulties and low self-esteem, but the Life Less Lived has shown me that even small victories like being able to catch a bus on your own or opening a bank account can mean the world to some people. Did I mention? – I LOVE this job too.

The Life Less Lived has taught me many lessons but mostly it has taught me to value small victories and appreciate the prosaic side of life. I can derive so much pleasure out of the blossom on a tree or cuddling a baby or sitting in my study and writing. Things that have no monetary value but are worth more than anything in the world.

> *To see a World in a Grain of Sand*
> *And a Heaven in a Wild Flower*
> *Hold Infinity in the palm of your hand*
> *And Eternity in an hour*
>
> From *'Auguries of Innocence'* by William Blake

I am sure I would have travelled far and wide had I not had my anxieties in tow, but would I have ever really experienced anything? Somehow my trip around America was so much more worthwhile because of the effort it took to get to the Golden Gate

Bridge, and my time in São Paulo was so much more real because I had a meltdown and the materially poor Brazilians were able to demonstrate to me what true human richness was all about.

In the last few years I have been spending a lot of time with my dad. He has been there for me through all my breakdowns and I will never forget the week he sat with me on suicide watch. He wanted me to be that successful accountant person in the parallel universe, and I often think I have let him down in that respect but I know he loves me better for the person I am now. Over recent times Dad has got older, and frailer and more poorly as the days go by. I love the Life Less Lived if for no other reason than it has given me valuable time to spend with him and appreciate his growing eccentricities. I don't want to spend thousands of pounds on the best care for him and not be there for him myself. We have laughed at his forgetfulness and I've read his mail to him and chatted about what's happening in *Corrie* and then he falls asleep and I'll sit and do some work until he wakes up and wants a cup of tea. There is nothing more precious or wonderful in the world than afternoons like that.

Does it really matter that my life didn't turn out exactly as planned? When in falling to pieces it actually turned out to be immeasurably more than I could ever have asked or imagined?

I've already talked in a previous chapter about how the Life Less Lived has brought me friends to whom I would never have given the time of day before. I've also explained how CBT has been invaluable to me in managing my anxiety and depression, but I have saved the best story until near the end.

Before I started my CBT sessions with Wanda I had the deep-routed belief that I was ugly and unlovable. My self-esteem was non-existent. It didn't really matter, I enjoyed solitude. I loved living on my own. So no one would find me attractive? I didn't want anyone! Of the many things I worked on with Wanda one of them was my feeling of unattractiveness towards men. We challenged the view that I was fat and repulsive. Wanda worked with me on not avoiding situations with men but approaching them with gentle curiosity.

Shortly after our sessions ended I received a message on social media from a friend of a friend asking me out for a meal. I panicked. I froze. He would be disgusted when he saw me. He'd think me a bore. But then I remembered my work with Wanda and I decided to take a risk and say yes. We changed the meal to a coffee and I put so many 'umms' and 'ahs' and 'I can only stay an hours' on it that he thought I wasn't interested and nearly didn't bother.

I didn't stay an hour. We sat chatting for over two hours and then went on for a meal and the whole date lasted more than eight hours, at the end of which he gave me a chaste kiss on the lips and I was left walking on air.

The mutual friend hadn't 'sold' me very well. She'd told him that I had borderline mental health issues. I laughed at this and told him that our mutual friend was wrong: there was nothing borderline about my mental health issues – they were fully blown, fully grown mental health issues and was he OK with that?

I might not normally have mentioned this on a first date but he brought it up and quite frankly when would be a good time to drop it into conversation? I welcome a time when people can talk openly about anxiety and depression without fear of rejection. As a society we're getting there but we're not there yet.

Not only was he OK with my confession but he loves me with all my brokenness and flaws. I even think he might adore me! Five years on he still treats me like a princess.

Mick is not a Barnaby. He would not have met my tick list pre-Life Less Lived. He is not ambitious, he's not a lawyer or an accountant (he has worked as a manual operator in factories most of his life), but he is funny and kind and intelligent. He too is on a journey, we are exploring the world together, making our own mistakes and growing and learning from them. He is worth a million Barnabys.

Let me tell you everything you will ever need to know about my husband. I can't do everything for my ageing dad. I work for one thing, and for another I am his daughter. Mick will catch two buses to see him and then two buses home again twice a week; he will help him in the shower, help him get dressed, be patient while my dad dithers and forgets what he wants to say; he'll handle bodily fluids that would make me heave and he doesn't ask for any payment apart from his bus fare. In eternity these are the things that will matter about a person, not their job description or the amount of their take home pay.

Our wedding day was one of the happiest of my life. All I cared about was that we were together with our friends. I didn't stress over the dress or the cake or the venue – none of that mattered. They were peripheral details compared with me and my new husband binding ourselves together at the altar. I didn't feel nervous when I got up to make my speech (public speaking has never been one of my phobias); what I said sums up all the joy and love that can be found down the twitchells and twisting roads of the Life Less Lived:

As I grew older I loved being single – I enjoyed spending time on my own – relished my independence and I always thought life was difficult enough without having a man to cope with as well! Then I met Mick – and everything changed!

As soon as I met him it really was like meeting my 'other-half'. It might have taken me over forty years to find him but I am so glad I didn't settle for second best along the way. I suddenly realised that with the right person beside you anything is possible. He is kind, sensitive, intelligent (he always beats me at quizzes), thoughtful, funny. He inspires me, he makes me laugh, he comforts me and he challenges me.

I want to say that Mick is my 'happy ending', but that's not true – he is my happy beginning. Because this is just the beginning of our life together and it's going to be an awfully big adventure!

Many times I think back to the hours and days when I wanted to end it all. How bleak and hopeless everything looked and how much effort it seemed to take to just hang on in there. Then I think about watching my goddaughters growing up; I think about taking one of them to Disney World; my amazing (frustrating) trip around America; the poverty and humanity I witnessed in Brazil; my wedding day and that awfully big adventure we are now on, and I am so, so grateful to my younger self for holding on for just another fifteen minutes, then another, then another until eventually the person I am today came out the other side.

Dark matter is needed to hold galaxies together. Your mind is a Galaxy. More dark than light. But the light makes it worthwhile.
From *The Humans* by Matt Haig

In fact it is more than these amazing milestones which make life so incredible. I think that when you are sitting alone in a room, really questioning what life is about, seriously considering that it is not worth the effort, then every ordinary, inconsequential moment after that is a bonus to be cherished. Looking out of my window now, to a very ordinary British street on a very normal May afternoon, I can see the sun speckled through golden leaves of the tree opposite. I can see a solitary fluffy cloud sailing carefree across a blue sky; I can see my neighbour's beautiful front garden filled with pretty coloured flora; I can feel the breeze cooling me through the window. Would I have really ever appreciated any of these small wonders if I hadn't once experienced such bleakness? Even though at the same time as I see this beauty, my stomach is churning for some inexplicable reason, my shoulders are tense and hunched, my head is beginning to throb from the constant barrage of 'what if' disaster scenarios that have been running through my mind all day. Despite all of this 'background noise' I can still look out of a window and appreciate what a really beautiful, wonderful and miraculous world it is.

CHAPTER TWELVE

Who Will Write the Next Chapter?

'There are better things ahead than we leave behind.'

C S Lewis

So what is next for me and you? Is the future bright? Have we got it all worked out? I don't know about you but as far as I'm concerned I know for certain there will be more anxiety and heartache ahead, but I'm not afraid of it anymore.

I began writing this book three years ago, shortly after leaving my umpteenth job due to anxiety, panic and depression. One day I was fine (well, as fine as I ever am), enjoying a cinema trip with my husband, the next day I was close to rock bottom, feeling suicidal and begging my GP for something to relieve the desperate pain and emptiness inside me. I was afraid, for the umpteenth time in my life, to leave the house, and I handed my notice in rather than face my line manager continuing to phone me. I was a mess.

And yet I wasn't quite at rock bottom, because I'd been down that road many times before, and each time I sink a little less and recover a little quicker. Over the past three years I have re-established my life on a more or less even keel. I have changed my medication, which has had a really positive effect on the physical symptoms of anxiety and my ability to control the panic. I have a new job that is flexible and more suited to my 'needs'. They don't expect me to work miracles, work extra hours without pay or get dressed up as a gnome to entertain elderly residents! When I told my new line manager about my anxiety history she was completely unfazed. 'That's just life,' she said. 'We'll deal with any problems as they arise.' I think my writing has been a huge help in keeping me grounded. Locking myself away in my study for a couple of hours of an evening is a great way to put my past and present worries into perspective.

I am not fooled, however – and I will never be fooled again – into believing that my days of doom, despair, abject fear and panic are behind me. I have fallen into that trap so many times that I now realise my mental ill health is so much a part of my make-up that I can only learn to love it. If I fight it and try to hide it then it just comes back bigger and stronger. If I acknowledge it and work with it, it is appeased and tends to live in the background noise of my daily life. I can't promise that I won't hide away in my room for days and weeks in years to come, but I know that each time it happens, my hideaways will be shorter and I will learn something else about myself and the world. Even in the depths of my future despairs I will know that I have travelled this road before and I always come out the other side.

So of course I will get ill again, but I am prepared. I have my toolbox ready and I use it regularly. I practise my tools, not as often or as well as I should, but I walk regularly, I try to eat healthily, I write, I read, I sleep. I take life one step at a time. I try to be mindful and practise my CBT. On the days and weeks that I do all this I cope better. When I get too busy or too cocky to keep the balance I tend to fall off the horse. When I do slip, when I get too stressed by work, or share a sneaky KFC bargain bucket with my husband, or fill my diary with too many engagements, I try above all to be gentle with myself. I am human. I am not perfect. I was never designed to be. I make mistakes. I am learning to live with that and love myself for it. In fact I am more than gentle. There are days after days after days that I give myself a huge pat on the back just for getting from one end of the day to the other without screaming, sobbing or throwing the towel in.

I live with mental illness but it doesn't have to define me. I am also a member of Mensa. I qualified as a chartered accountant and now work as a bookkeeper/accountant for small charities. I am a writer, a wife, a (fairy) godmother. I am a qualified teacher. I am a survivor. My brother recently asked me if it was necessary to talk about mental health because nowadays everyone is open and honest about it. Are they? Really? True, we don't live in a Victorian era where crazy relatives are confined to attic rooms or asylums, and we have come a long way since the days of my paternal grandma, who didn't leave the house for a decade but was just described as being 'a bit hysterical'. But even so, many people still feel the need to keep their mental illness a secret. I'm still amazed by the number of people I come across who will suddenly open up to me about their own demons when I am honest about mine. As I said in my very first chapter, we are all flashing, but that is still seen as a weakness rather than an inevitable part of modern life.

Don't even get me started on the media and popular press who love to vilify people with mental health issues. If I were to brutally stab my neighbours (highly unlikely, I should add) the headline is bound to read MADWOMAN GOES ON KILLING SPREE, the editorials would ask why I was allowed to live in the community, why wasn't I sectioned; they would question NHS policy, they would interview my doctors. They would research and find other cases where people with a mental health diagnosis had committed a crime, and they would sense a pattern. I doubt very much they would look at how many accountants had gone on a killing spree, or contact Mensa to see if there was a link between a high IQ and a tendency to violent crime. No, many people still equate mental illness with violence. For so many it is something to fear in others, something disturbing and distasteful that might possibly be catching.

> In 2009, the total population in England and Wales was just over **43 million**. It is estimated that about one in six of the adult population will have a significant mental health problem at any one time (more than **7 million** people). Given this number and the **50–70** cases of homicide a year involving people known to have a mental health problem at the time of the murder, clearly the statistics data do not support the sensationalised media coverage about the danger that people with mental health problems present to the community.
>
> www.timetochange.org.uk

Yes, thankfully attitudes are changing, but there is still a long way to go. And change is necessary because one in four people will experience mental ill health in any one year. That's a lot of people walking around feeling like they've got some terrible, dirty secret to hide.

After my last ignominious exit from a job, the one described in Chapter 8, I decided enough was enough. I would tell any future employers at interview, or at least before I took the post. My friends were horrified (good, supportive, open-to-mental-health-issues friends, I should add). 'You *can't* mention it at interview!' they counselled. 'You won't get the job!'

I have finally learned that an interview is a two-way process and I am interviewing the employer every bit as much as they are interviewing me. If their attitude to mental health isn't supportive I don't want the job. It's a risk, but then again so is taking a job with no idea of how they will respond to a panic attack. I have tried this twice so far and both times, not only was I pleased with the responses, I was offered both jobs. The first was a temporary part-time job (my way of regaining my confidence after my latest period of ill health), the second the job I have now. I will never again work for an organisation that isn't supportive of mental health. I don't want to be ridiculed or threatened with disciplinary action because I have panic attacks. I want to work in a supportive environment where I don't need to get panicky, or if I do I know that my colleagues and superiors will have my back. That's the way to avoid long periods of sick leave or frequent job changes. Employers with this attitude are admittedly few and far between, but things are changing.

Tips from my Toolbox: Build your own box of tools

As the Roman poet Lucretius once said '*quod ali cibus est aliis fuat acre venenum*,' or to those of you not fluent in Latin 'what is food for one man may be bitter poison to others.' Through the toolbox sections of this book I have tried to give you an insight into what has worked for me in managing my anxiety and depression. They are the meat of my coping strategies, if you like. I would hope none of them would turn out to be bitter poison for you, but I am sure that they won't appeal to everyone and certainly won't work for all of you.

My final tip, then, is to find what works for you and use it! Daily! Use it when you are well in order that you are prepared when you are low. Get prepared, get 'tooled up', you never know when your next bad day will come, but having these tools to hand and easily memorable will really help when you are facing the precipice.

So, a few final tips on tips! First, you've probably realised by now that I don't believe there is one miracle cure out there. You will get better and learn to live with yourself through a combination of tools and strategies. Some you may grow weary of, some you may grow out of, some you may return to like an old friend who chats to you like you've never been apart even though you haven't seen them for several years. Find a set of therapies, books or ways of life which help you and support you.

Second, don't be fooled by charlatans; you shouldn't have to spend a fortune on good mental health or feeling good about life. Pretty much every single tool I've talked about is free or relatively cheap. There are an abundance of self-help books in every library I have visited, a walk in the fresh air costs nothing. In the UK we are lucky to have the NHS and you can get support and medication from your GP for the price of a prescription charge. You can get counselling and CBT on the National Health (although I would suggest it's not widely enough available and you may have to wait for it). Private therapists are of course available if you have the money, but do your research before parting with any cash. Your GP will probably know of some reputable practitioners locally.

I've said it before but I'll say it again: beware of toxic tools! Not everything that makes you feel good in the short term is healthy in the long term. Ask yourself, is this really doing me any good? I tend to find that toxic tools are the ones that have become habits that I can't easily give up or they are the things my subconscious reaches for in a moment of stress. A simple example, I feel bad, I hate myself, chocolate will cheer me up. Yes, I'll buy a big bar of Dairy Milk, I'll only have a square, or two, or… oh, go on then I might as well finish off the whole bar now! Afterwards I feel sick, my sugar levels go through the roof and I get a quick high but then my sugar levels plummet and I feel low and depressed. I'm angry at myself for eating a whole bar of chocolate but also because the sugar is playing havoc with my inner chemicals. If I keep doing this (and I do, believe me I do)

I get fatter, more lethargic, less able to cope with life's ups and downs. It becomes a habit, I do it more often, then I can't stop.

Maybe I'm exaggerating slightly, or maybe not so much; it's the cumulative effect that can be harmful. One chocolate bar won't hurt you, but eating chocolate every day will affect your health both physically and mentally. Toxic tools don't help you but then neither does it help to beat yourself up about them: paradoxically that seems to only make you want to use them more... and if someone else challenges your toxic tools – well, we all know that's like a red rag to a bull! All I would say is look at what you are using to cope with your stress, anxiety and depression and ask two questions: 'Is this helpful in the long term?' and 'Am I controlling the tool or is the tool controlling me?'

The power is in the choices you make every day.
Sign outside YMCA Nottingham

Toxicity can extend to people and if anything can bring you down, it's a toxic person. I talked in Chapter 3 about how having a mental illness has shown me who my friends are... and who they definitely aren't! When you are vulnerable and low you need people around who are going to be strong and supportive, not those who are going to prey on your vulnerability. They may not be doing this deliberately or maliciously, they may be struggling with their own inner terrors, but you can't do anything to help them if you aren't feeling strong and stable yourself. I have lost many 'friends' over the years. In some cases I was probably the toxic person and my friend couldn't cope with my demands; in others I just got scared and ran away. However, there have been times when I have had to take a good hard look at a relationship and make the decision that I am not going to get better with these people around me. It's a hard decision to make.

As a child, if I ever fell out with a friend, my mum would always, always without fail say, 'Oh what have you done to upset them now?' Always it was assumed that I was the person in the wrong, that I had somehow failed to maintain the friendship. As an adult this led my subconscious to hold on to all friendships at any cost. If someone moved on or moved away or found me disagreeable I must have done something wrong. It took me a long time to learn to choose my friends wisely.

Another revelation to me in a similar vein was that I am a natural introvert. I get strength from being alone. The more time I can have alone the better; if I don't have time alone I go, quite literally, mad. I used to think this was just a symptom of my social phobia, that it was part of what was 'wrong' with me, but then I was introduced to Myers-Briggs personality profiling (www.myersbriggs.org) and I realised that quite a large proportion of the population want and need time alone more than they need time around others. There is a lot of talk in society about loneliness, but is there a word for the opposite of loneliness? When you've overloaded on people and long for solitude? I know that I need to be on my own, so a large part of my strategy for staying well is to make sure I spend enough time on my own. It is as important to me as eating; I could never have too much solitude… and maybe you're like that too and need to prioritise time for yourself?

Or maybe you're not? Maybe you're screaming at me right now because you are lonely and have nowhere to turn? That's probably because you are an extrovert and need other people to give you strength and improve your mood, in which case I would urge you to join a club or a support group or an online chatroom. It will take time to meet new people and to grow a friendship but it will be a positive challenge which will in time bear fruit.

And so these are my tips, and of course there are others. There are things I haven't tried yet, or things I just didn't have time or space to write about. For some people animals bring great comfort and companionship, a long soak in a hot bath can work wonders and I love to use aromatherapy to calm my mind. Walking by the sea or through a field is another option, or having a massage. I find cleaning massively therapeutic; it burns energy, gets you moving and the feeling of a clean room or fresh sheets is divine (of course not everyone shares my enthusiasm about cleaning – like I say, you choose what works for you).

Over to You: Build your own Toolbox: A summary

- Take small steps, only as big as you can manage, get through the next minute, the next task, one small step after one small step.
- Get help from a professional, let them advise you on therapy and medication – but do your research as well, GPs only know so much, psychiatrists know more but no one knows you as well as you do.
- Look for the positive when everything feels negative, write it down, keep writing it down, every day. On your dark days read through your list and remember the way these things made you smile or feel positive.
- Accept yourself, accept your feelings, don't try and battle and berate yourself for being you. You are what you are and you feel what you feel; acceptance will get you much further along the road of healing than denying yourself.
- Be gentle and kind to yourself, put that big stick you keep beating yourself with away.
- Read self-help books but use your library or you could end up spending thousands. Take what's useful for you and ignore the rest.

- Be mindful, live in the moment, be aware of what is happening now. Don't dwell on the past, or worry about the future (but if you do – don't feel bad – just gently bring your mind back to the present).
- Listen to music.
- Develop a GSOH, Good Sense of Humour. Learn to laugh at yourself, learn to laugh even when you are crying. See the lighter side of life.
- Hold on to that tiny mustard seed of faith.
- Take up an engrossing hobby such as photography, singing, writing, something that will focus your attention away from your inner worries and woes.
- Eat healthily, plenty of fruit and veg, not so much processed food and even fewer artificial sugars and sweeteners (but allow yourself the occasional treat).
- Get moving, do something you enjoy, get the endorphins (happy chemicals) flowing around your body.
- Sleep (sleep is my answer to just about any situation!).
- Give Cognitive Behavioural Therapy (CBT) a try. It's not for everyone but it is the single most helpful thing I have ever done in terms of improving my mental health. There are also other types of therapies out there that might be more suitable to your situation – your GP should be able to advise you.

I hope you will find something useful here, and even if you don't I hope it will spur you on to discover what does work for you. Depression and anxiety can be managed sufficiently to live a fulfilling and productive life. I am quite at ease with the fact that people will ignore or pooh-pooh my ideas, but if there is one thing that I would urge, beg, plead with every one of you to do, if you only take one thing away from this whole book it is to be gentle and kind to yourself. Time and time again I meet people who spend hours of time and endless energy berating and criticising themselves. Often they are the people who least need such flagellation. I can't put it any better than that famous poem Desiderata, so I will end my tips section with an excerpt.

Good luck.

Beyond a wholesome discipline, be gentle with yourself. You are a child of the universe no less than the trees and the stars; you have a right to be here.

And whether or not it is clear to you, no doubt the universe is unfolding as it should.

From *Desiderata* by Max Ehrmann

* * *

And so continues the Life Less Lived, and I love it more and more each day. Every so often life throws us a curve ball that knocks us off course but that curve ball can lead to wonderful, unexpected places. John Lennon said, 'Life is what happens while you are busy making other plans?' He knew what he was talking about, but what he didn't say was how gloriously deep and fulfilling that life can be, better than all our plans and dreams.

'Life is what happens while you are busy making other plans.'
John Lennon

The latest curve ball for our family has been my dad's declining health. My relationship with my dad is infinitely better because of my mental ill health; getting to know him better has been one of the great things about the Life Less Lived. In good days and bad, for over forty years my dad has been there for me. It was always him who nursed me when I was sick at five years old. It was him who drove my drunk friends home from parties when we were too young to drink; it was him who travelled all the way from London to Nottingham in the middle of the night to tell me I had passed my accountancy exams; it was him who helped me out numerous times when the month was longer than the money, and he has always, always been there as my rock when I've failed and fallen time and time again.

The depth of our relationship has been cemented by my weaknesses much more often than my strengths. Therefore it was a recent pleasure and a privilege to drive over and see him when he'd had a fall, to sit in hospital waiting rooms when he wasn't sure why he was there, to hold his hand when he was dizzy and needed to lean on me. I developed the patience to explain seventeen times in one day how to turn the TV on, I loved the times we sat and watched *Corrie* (and he dozed off and missed all the good bits). I can even laugh at the time when we went to see the GP and he swore blind that he never fell over, even though everyone, from his neighbours to the nurses in hospital to anyone who took one look at him, knew that he did. This is the Life Less Lived. On the life I'd planned I wouldn't have had time for my dad now and I would have been much poorer because of it.

Exactly three weeks after I'd finished the first draft of this book, that particular curve ball swung back and hit me in the face when my dad was rushed into hospital, where he was to spend the final six weeks of his life. If ever I have needed my tools and my support mechanisms it is now. Those last six weeks were imperfect. He wanted to be at home. A private man who craved solitude and loved silence he was forced to lie in a ward of other sick old men who swore at the nurses and who often cried out, 'Don't let me die here.' The Italian man in the next bed seemed to have eight or nine guests round his bed every afternoon, including an old woman with Alzheimer's who decided to go rooting through my dad's possessions for no particular reason. If any time in my dad's life was Less Lived, it was these final hours.

Yet there was so much to love and cherish and celebrate as well. Dad was declining before our eyes but, until he lost the power of speech, we still had much to laugh about. I told him I loved him and was proud of him and tried to hide my tears. I saw the heroism and kindness of NHS staff. It was a privilege and honour to show a dying man how precious and wonderful he was, and always will be. I grew closer to my brother and my husband, as we shared the grief and the joys those final weeks brought.

Nothing about his last days went right. Every treatment they tried saw him decline further until the consultant finally agreed we could bring him home to die in peace. We got as far as having the hospital bed delivered, we were hours away from transporting him home, but he was fading away so rapidly that the consultant said it would be cruel to move him.

So I spent my last evening with him trying to shut out the rest of the ward. I was oblivious to the other patients' moans and the cleaners' idle chit-chat. It was the furthest place from perfect, it was everything my dad had never wanted, but it was all we had. He didn't wake up. I sat beside him writing down every memory I had of him, afraid I would forget. Every so often I would talk to him and play country music on my phone, which I rested on his pillow. Then I kissed him goodbye and prayed that there was a very special place being prepared for him in paradise. A glorious and heavenly surprise where he would be free from pain and confusion and he could watch Sky Sports around the clock without ever getting tired!

That evening was not how I wanted it to be. It was the Life Less Lived.

He died the next morning. We were driving to the hospital when we got the call to say he was going. We arrived ten minutes later, five minutes after he had passed away. It wasn't how I planned it. There was no happy ending. I chose to see his body, thinking there might be some comfort there but he didn't look peaceful or at rest, the way some people describe. He just looked dead. And empty.

At that moment a tsunami of grief hit me and threatened to engulf me. All thoughts of tools and techniques went out the window. I didn't think I would survive and yet, paradoxically, I know I will. At least until it is my turn to lie on a hospital bed as my own life ebbs away. The Life Less Lived is full of grief, disappointments and longing. In months to come there will be lessons I have to learn from this latest chapter, but for now I just have to hold the grief and emptiness, cumbersome and unwieldy as they are, until I can let them go or find a safe place for them somewhere in my soul.

In the days left to me I will take time to look around, I will take time to rest, I will approach the next twist in the road with gentle curiosity and I will enjoy the ride for what it is, not for where it can get me, even if the ride takes me to places I don't want to go. I am more grateful than I could ever believe for all I have. I am glad I have lived to see this life because there have been months and years when I wished that life would stop and for that I now feel ashamed (and very glad that whoever is out there listening in the universe ignored that particular plea).

I will endeavour to know my limits but that won't stop me dreaming and planning new adventures. I won't let it stop me loving life with all its flaws and imperfections. I still work with young people and hopefully make a difference to one or two of their lives, but I'm big enough to admit that working as a secondary science teacher with a class of teenage delinquents equipped with Bunsen burners and acid, or with teenagers who are on drugs and have been expelled from every other educational establishment, are probably not the best jobs for me.

I still work, I don't earn a fortune, I'm not a CEO, but I enjoy my job, I like my colleagues and I make a difference to weary volunteers who work at the grass roots of society. I have time to spend with my family but still manage to eke out enough solitude to keep myself sane. I have a few close friends but, although I try to be friendly with everyone I meet, I don't go out of my way to extend my friendship group. My relationships have been grounded in shared troubles and I would choose quality over quantity any time. As the old saying goes, I'd rather have four quarters than 100 pennies any day. I hope, God willing, to travel some more, maybe even to Brazil, but on my journey I will take care of myself and have plenty of breaks to stop and look at the view. I am not cut out for ten-week camping trips with strangers. I know that now!

And so what about you? Who will write the next chapter of your life? What will it involve? Are you prepared for the twists and turns in the plot? Will the star of the show (you) be the genuine thing or a cheap imitation of yourself, designed to live up to other people's expectations but showing nothing of your true inner strength? Will it be a stunning in-depth performance or a weak recital where you are just reading someone else's script? Who will be the supporting cast? Who are the villains who might try and throw your performance off track? Most of all, who will be the director of your destiny? Will you be in control of your mental health or will your mental health be controlling you?

I didn't set out to write this book because I know all the answers. Far from it – I've just about worked out the questions! I wrote it because I want other people to feel comfortable in their own skin, especially people with mental health issues but also everyone who has found themselves on the Life Less Lived, because something came along and changed their plans. I want people to see the joy and love that is hidden all around us, even at the bedside of a dying man who has meant the world to you for over forty years. I want people to Love the Life Less Lived in the same way I do. I hope I will inspire people to write their own story, past, present and future, whether in creative arts or deeds of kindness or just by encouraging others who are finding life difficult. Everyone has their own unique set of skills to bring to the world. I hope I will encourage people to discover their strengths and be kind about their own failings in the same way my old friend Angela encouraged me all those months ago. I want to support people to find their own ways of coping with this thing we call life and above all to welcome and love the Life Less Lived.

If you think that's all very well but it doesn't apply to me, remember those people in Chapter 9 who have accomplished great things in spite of or because of their mental health issues. Remember me feeling sorry for myself at the start of this book, OK so I haven't achieved greatness quite yet, but I've written a book! Whatever is holding you down at the moment doesn't have to be a barrier to your hopes, dreams or aspirations. Yes it may take more planning, you may have more setbacks than the average person, life may throw a few more curve balls at you to scupper your plans, but therein lies the beauty of the Life Less Lived.

Through the difficulties you will learn your strengths, you will have a greater story to tell – and how much greater the joy, how fantastic the feeling of success when you catch sight of your own personal Golden Gate Bridge, write your own book, or accomplish that dream that has always been your destiny since you set out on this road. This is your Life Less Lived: it is the only one you will get, so love it and live it with all your heart.

'All will be well
... and all will be well
... and all manner of things will be well.'

Julian of Norwich

Further Reading

This is just a very small sample of the myriad of other books that you might find useful.

Quick reads

Collard, Dr Patrizia, *The Little Book of Mindfulness*
(Gaia, 2014, ISBN 978-1-85675-353-1)
Curtiss, A B, *The Little Chapel That Stood*
(Old Castle Publishing, 2003, ISBN 978-0932529770)
Goodwin, Daisy, *101 Poems That Could Save Your Life*
(HarperCollins, 2003, ISBN 978-0002570725)
Johnstone, Matthew, *I Had a Black Dog* (Robinson, 2007,
ISBN 978-1845295899)
Wilson, Paul, *The Little Book of Calm* (Penguin, 1999,
ISBN 978-0-140-28526-0)

Books by people who've been there

Haig, Matt, *Reasons to Stay Alive* (Canongate, 2015,
ISBN 978-1782116820)
Nouwen, Henri J M, *The Inner Voice of Love* (Darton,
Longman & Todd, 2014, ISBN 978-0232530780)

More in-depth reading

Fundamental Facts About Mental Health, 2015 – Document available for free from the Mental Health Foundation's website: www.mentalhealth.org.uk.
Gilbert, Paul, *Overcoming Depression* (Robinson, 2009, ISBN 978-1849010665)
Kennerley, Helen, *Overcoming Anxiety* (Robinson, 2014, ISBN 978-1849018784)
McRaney, David, *You Can Beat Your Brain* (Oneworld Publications, 2013, ISBN 978-1780743745)
Pittman, Catherine M & Karle, Elizabeth M, *Rewire your Anxious Brain* (New Harbinger, 2015, ISBN 978-1626251137)
Willson, Rob & Branch, Rhena, *Cognitive Behavioural Therapy for Dummies* (For Dummies, 2010, ISBN 978-0470665411)

Other useful books

Helfgott, Gillian, *Love You to Bits and Pieces: Life with David Helfgott* (Penguin, 1997, ISBN 978-0140265460)
Heppell, Michael, *Flip It: How to Get the Best Out of Everything* (Pearson Life, 2011, ISBN 978-0273761211)
Hoff, Benjamin, *The Tao of Pooh* (Egmont, 2003, ISBN 978-1405204262)
Hurnard, Hannah, *Hinds' Feet on High Places* (Kingsway Publications, 2001, ISBN 978-0854769834)
Joseph, Martyn, *Notes on Words* – Available as a PDF download from www.martynjoseph.net/shop
Mortimore, Denise, *The Complete Illustrated Guide to Nutritional Healing* (Element, 1998, ISBN 978-1862041752)
Parks, Rosa with Haskins, Jim, *Rosa Parks: My Story* (Puffin, 1999, ISBN 978-0141301204)
Ten Boom, Corrie, *The Hiding Place* (Hodder & Stoughton, 2004, ISBN 978-0340863534)
Weathers, Beck, *Left for Dead* (Sphere, 2015, ISBN 978-0751561890)